To Don!
Best Wishes,
Jerome Art

Also by Jerome Arthur

The Death of Soc Smith

A Novella

Jerome Arthur

The Death of Soc Smith

Published by Jerome Arthur
P.O. Box 818
Santa Cruz, California 95061
831-425-8818
www.JeromeArthurNovelist.com
Jerome@JeromeArthurNovelist.com

Acknowledgments

Special thanks to Don Rothman and Kimberley Peake for editorial assistance and Jim Mullen for the cover design.

One

The low tide would be -0.7 at five to six that Saturday morning in April, and if he was going surfing, Soc Smith wanted to be in the water by a quarter to six, so he was up at five o'clock. He had checked the surf the morning before on his way to work, and there had been a decent swell with a few sets coming through, so he was hoping for the same today. He'd loaded his board and wet-suit into the Woody the night before, so all he had to do in the morning was drive down to the beach, and if it looked good, put his suit on and throw his stick in the water. Since he didn't have to go to work that day, he could stay in the water for as long as the sets kept coming through. Friday night he'd told his wife, Jayne, that he'd help her in the yard in the afternoon. However, if he surfed till noon, he'd be too tired for any yard work. Soc didn't have the pep he'd had as a teenager and young man.

The Death of Soc Smith

There had been a gentle sprinkle the night before, so the lawns and streets were glistening as he drove to the beach. There was only a scattering of clouds, and they were moving slowly east, leaving the sky clear. Day was just barely breaking, and his headlights cast two narrow, shiny funnels onto the pavement in front of him. When he got to the cliff, Jesse Vaca was pulling his Chevy truck into a parking space just ahead of him. Jesse's board was in its bag in the pickup bed. Soc pulled in beside him, and they got out of their cars together and walked over to the edge of the cliff to look at the waves. As early and damp as it was, it was quite warm.

"So, wha'da yuh think?" Soc asked as they stood gazing out at the surf under the dawning sky. Nobody was in the water, but a few other surfers were standing on the cliff checking it out, too.

"Not lookin' too bad," Jesse said. "I'm go'n'a go out."

"Yeah? Doesn't look that good to me," Soc said. "Wasn't too bad yesterday. Better'n this, for sure."

"Look at this set. Some nice little ankle snappers there."

The mountain ridge across the bay to the east was beginning to show some color.

The sun peaked over the horizon at the slot where the Salinas River flowed into the bay. Tiny, one-foot waves creamed into the beach below. The tide was so low that there was sand fifty yards out from the stairs. One surfer was making his way down the steps. At the bottom he attached his leash and walked on the sand along the cliff until he was knee-deep in the water. He slid onto his board when it got to his upper thighs. Soc and Jesse watched as he paddled to the outside.

"That's it. I'm goin' out," said Jesse.

"Think I'm go'n'a pass."

"I'm go'n'a give it a try. Nothin' else, I can just go out and paddle around."

"Hey, go for it. See yuh later."

It wasn't worth it for Jesse to drive all the way into town and not get in the water. He lived nine miles up the mountain at the upper end of San Lorenzo Valley. Even when it was completely flat, Jesse would get in and, as he put it, "paddle around."

Backing out of his parking space, Soc saw him take his board out of the back of his pickup and remove the bag. He headed out to Steamer Lane to see what it looked like out there. The waves at Indicators were a little bigger than they were at Cowell's. He'd tried to surf there once, but it was way too big for his liking. He went over the falls on the first

8

wave he'd tried to catch. It was only a chest-high wave, and he'd caught many that size at Cowell's, but they weren't nearly as fast as the one he'd caught at Indicators. He wiped out good. He was under water a long time and going through the spin cycle, and when he got out, he started throwing up. It scared him, and he hadn't gotten back in the water for another couple weeks after that.

After he rounded the point at Indicators, he could see that the waves at First Peak and Middle Peak were shoulder high and looking glassy. He'd never surfed these waves. They were way too big and way too fast for him. The guys who surfed them were young, aggressive kids. Too competitive, no fun. Many's the time when he'd stood on the cliff at the point and heard some young guy in the water hollering an obscenity at some other young guy for some silly infraction the latter didn't even know he'd committed. And on the nicest of days, too. He rounded the point and was on his way back home.

He pulled the car into the garage. An old rusty hamster cage sat on top of a case of motor oil on the floor against the back wall. He inched in slowly until the rubber ball that hung from the rafters touched his windshield. He got his board and wetsuit out and stored them on the rack and in the cabinet he'd made especially for them.

It was almost six-thirty, and Jayne was just getting out of bed. He went into the bedroom through the sliding glass door off the patio. He took his shoes off, put on his fleece-lined slippers, and went through the living room and out the front door to pick up the morning newspaper. He tossed the paper onto the dining room table as he went into the kitchen and started boiling water for a cup of hot-spiced cider. He warmed up a couple of bran muffins in the microwave and used the leftover-spiced cider water to make a cup of instant oatmeal. After he got everything set up on the dining room table, he sat down and spread out the front page of the newspaper, and, as he ate, he skimmed that section.

By now Jayne was bustling around the kitchen brewing a pot of coffee. She kissed Soc's bald spot as she went to Caroline's bedroom to turn her computer on. She communicated by email every morning with their daughter, Caroline, on the east coast and her cousin in Portland, Oregon.

"No surf?" She asked.

"Nothing worth getting wet for."

"Oh, I'm sorry. I know how antsie you get when there's no surf."

The Death of Soc Smith

When she returned to the kitchen, she put some food out for the cats, filled her coffee cup and went back to her computer. The cats were all that was left at home. Caroline was a college junior in Massachusetts.

Soc didn't really *read* the newspaper. He only skimmed the headlines of the first section. If he saw a story that interested him, or if he knew the person the story was about, he'd read a paragraph or two to get the gist. The only kinds of stories that he read all the way through were stories about local surfing. Every year when the Cold Water Classic was held, Soc read all the stories that were written about it to see how well they matched up with the actual event, the last day of which he always attended. Then he'd move on to the last two pages for the political cartoon, letters to the editor, again looking for familiar names at the end of each one, and the vital statistics. He skimmed these religiously every day looking for familiar names among the births and divorces. When he'd go to the obituaries, he only read the ones of the people who were younger than he was, curious to know what killed them. Soc looked at the first obituary in the upper left-hand corner of the page, and to his astonishment he read:

Jerome Arthur

SOCRATES SMITH

No services will be held for Socrates Smith who died Friday after a brief illness. He was 53.

A native of Los Angeles, he lived in Santa Cruz for twenty years. He was employed by a Scotts Valley electronics firm.

He is survived by his wife Jayne Smith and his daughter Caroline Smith.

Contributions are preferred to The Surfrider Foundation.

He couldn't believe his eyes. At first there was the surge of excitement at seeing his name in the newspaper, but the delight was immediately tempered by the awareness that where he was seeing it was in the obituaries. He was so shocked that he couldn't tell Jayne what he was reading. All he could do was stare at it and chuckle. He wanted to call out to her but couldn't. He was stuck somewhere between laughter and a heart-sinking feeling that something was very wrong, and he might not be able to fix it. Finally, he caught his breath and said,

"Hey, Babe. You might wan'a take a look at this."

The Death of Soc Smith

She must have heard some urgency in his voice because when she got to the dining room table, the casual Saturday morning look on her face had changed to panic.

"What's wrong, Honey?"

"Check out my obituary."

She quickly read through the item in the paper.

"My God, Soc," she said. "What do you suppose it means? It's got'a be a mistake. Let's get that newspaper on the phone and find out what the big idea is."

Just such innocent statements from Jayne were what endeared her to him. Whenever there was something that was seriously wrong, she was going to make it right, and she'd take on a determined little-girl-we-can-conquer-the-world attitude, and by God it'll get straightened out, or else!

"Have to wait till Monday," Soc said. He was talking a lot calmer than he actually felt. "Probably nobody there today. I don't believe this. Who, do you suppose, wrote that little blurb? Must be a practical joke. Someone's messin' with me. And then maybe not. Maybe it's for real. But how could it be?"

That's what he said, but he wasn't sure he believed any of it. When he stopped talking, he realized that he'd been rambling, and he knew it was only because he was confused and unsure of what was going on. Then he began to wonder if Jayne detected his un-certainty, but he couldn't tell, so he just kept to himself as he got into the comics.

Two

The phone started ringing less than ten minutes after he'd read the item in the paper. The first call was from Roland, Soc's closest friend. When Soc answered it, there was silence at the other end for a few seconds, and then Roland responded with surprise at the sound of his voice. It took him about five minutes to explain to Roland that it was a mistake and he'd get things straightened out on Monday morning.

"Scared the shit out'a me, man," Roland said. "Just talked to yuh on Tuesday, and yuh sounded okay then. Couldn't imagine what you could've come down with."

"Hey, let me tell yuh," Soc said, "I got scared, too, when I read it. It's either a mistake or somebody's playing a grim practical joke. 'Cause one thing's for sure. I ain't dead."

"So, wha'd'yuh think's goin' on. If it ain't a mistake or a joke, what else could it be?"

"Beats the shit outa' me. First thing Monday morning, I'm goin' down to the paper. They got'a know *something*. Like I said before, I'm not dead."

"All right! Now you're talkin'. It's still weird, but we got'a do something to take your mind off it. How 'bout we go play a round up at De Laveaga. That'll do it."

"Sounds like a hell of a good idea, but I can't today. I'm helpin' Jayne in the yard later. Got'a mow the lawns and prep the beds so she can plant some flowers."

"That may be better therapy for you. Don't have to think about anything. Probably wouldn't be able concentrate on your game. Me neither. Maybe next week, huh? We haven't golfed for quite a while, man."

"You're right. It's been a while. Maybe next Saturday."

"Okay," Roland said. "We'll be in touch. And you take care. I'm feelin' kinda' creepy about all this shit."

"Yeah, me too."

As soon as Soc replaced the receiver in its cradle, it rang again, but he didn't pick up. Instead, he grabbed the sports section, which he hadn't read yet, and walked away

The Death of Soc Smith

from the ringing phone, leaving Jayne to answer it. He wanted to run some hot water and soak in the tub. As he headed toward the bathroom, he heard over his shoulder that it was Betty, Jayne's commuting partner. Before he got out of earshot, he heard Jayne explaining to her that the obituary was a mistake.... He had to get away from the phone and get relaxed before doing battle with the yard.

When he got into the tub, he lay back in the steaming water and propped up his paperback copy of *The Lady in the Lake* and started to read. The tub wasn't a hot tub with jets; it was a comfortable old-time claw foot bathtub. Soc had rigged a sheet metal circle with a hole drilled in the top over the drain vent. This allowed him to fill the tub a good three inches higher than before. When he lay flat on his back with his knees bent, he was completely submerged except for his knees, his head, and his hands, which held the book. He could almost get his knees under water too if he crossed his legs yoga-fashion and flattened them out. When he had time like he had today, time gained (or lost depending on how you looked at it) because he hadn't gone surfing, he'd stay in the tub for almost an hour. When he first got in the tub, the water was steaming hot; by the time he got out, it was still quite warm.

…wonder if the people at work read that obituary…if they did, i wonder what they're thinking…got'a call 'em on monday morning before i go to the newspaper…tell 'em it was a mistake…tell 'em i'll be late 'cause I got'a straighten it out…snap out of it, man…nothin' you can do right now….

He could hear the phone ringing in the other room. Always twice, and then Jayne's muffled voice explaining the obituary. She'd hang up, and it'd ring again and so on.

…lota' people've seen the obit….

He read his book as these thoughts skipped through his head. He went back to the previous page and found the last sentence he'd remembered reading. He started reading again from there, concentrating hard, and then he was locked into the story and he read steadily for the next forty minutes, following Philip Marlowe from Hollywood out to the San Bernardino mountains and back to Bay City.

…must be a fictitious name for malibu or someplace like that….

Soc stepped out of the warm water and onto the cool tile floor. He went into the bedroom with the towel wrapped around his

The Death of Soc Smith

waist. It was getting on to late morning and the phone had stopped ringing. Jayne came into the bedroom as he was getting dressed.

"Who all called?" he asked.

"Oh, just about everybody we know: the Rafes, the Woodses and the Brankes. I got tired of explaining, so I finally silenced the ringer. Let the voice mail pick it up. I've got things to do; I can't be answering the phone all day."

"Anybody from work call?"

"Uh, uh. I guess none of those people read the newspaper, or at least they don't read the obituaries. Why are you putting on your good clothes? Don't you remember that we're working in the yard today?"

"Oh, yeah, I remember, but I thought I'd take a bike ride downtown before we get started. Finishing up the book I'm reading pretty soon, so I'm go'n'a go to the bookstore and get another one. I shouldn't be gone more'n an hour or so. Okay?"

"Sure. I've still got some things to do inside before I go outside."

Soc finished getting dressed and went into the bathroom to brush his teeth. Jayne went back to the kitchen. Soc followed her after he'd finished brushing. He wiped the dishes dry as she washed them. When that chore was finished, he went out to the garage and took his mountain bike down off the hooks it hung from in the rafters. As he passed the house on his way downtown, the front door was open, and he could hear the whirring of the vacuum cleaner. The cats were on the windowsills on each side of the front door.

He made one quick cruise of the Mall and locked his bike up near the end and walked back to Logos bookstore. He didn't run into anybody he knew, and he was glad of it, because he didn't want to spend half his day trying to convince people that he wasn't dead. He went straight to the "mysteries" section of the bookstore. It was a used bookstore, so he always got good deals on his reading material. He was liking the Chandler novel, so he looked for another one. There were a couple. He picked *The Big Sleep*, which only cost him seventy-five cents, half the cover price. He put the book in the waist pack with his wallet and keys. Then he crossed the street and walked up the Mall on the other side to where his bike was locked.

Back on his bike he decided to go take another look at the surf, so he pedaled out there and wasn't surprised to see that it was looking like Lake Tahoe: flat, that is. There were no surfers in the water. Jesse's

The Death of Soc Smith

truck was gone from where it had been parked. He continued pedaling around to check out the point. It was the same there as it had been earlier in the morning. Chest high sets were coming all the way through Middle Peak, but they petered out before they got to Indicators.

He rode around the point, and as he made the turn, he encountered the little white haired, red faced old man he'd seen a few years ago lawn bowling in the park along the river levee. Those afternoons of watching old people, men and women, dressed in white outfits, white all the way down to the shoes, were quiet comfort for him. He remembered thinking of them as weird dreams. It was like watching a scene from heaven where old folks were floating around in an elysian nirvana, contented, lawn bowling.

And there Soc was looking right at one. He was surprised the guy was still alive. It was fifteen years since Soc had seen him lawn bowling, and he was old then.

...at least he isn't puffing on a cigarette like he used to out on that lawn bowling court...i wonder if he still bowls....

A little after Soc passed the old man, he got off the bike path, crossed the street and headed through Lighthouse Field just past Its Beach and was on his way home.

When he got there, Jayne was putting on her gardening clothes. The mail had arrived in his absence, and Jayne told him to look at a letter she got from the county. When he picked it up off the dining room table, he was looking at a copy of his own official death certificate from the County Office of Vital Statistics.

...now it's really getting ridiculous...one more stop monday morning at the county building....

He went into the bedroom and changed into his gardening clothes, and they were ready to go to work.

Three

Soc mowed and edged the lawn while Jayne weeded the beds. When they finished, he filled three plastic trash bags with what she pulled out of the beds. They quit working and started cleaning up at four o'clock. They'd been working straight since one o'clock and they were both tired. Once again, they discussed the possibility of hiring someone to at least mow and edge the lawns. This was a subject that came up often of late. Soc was tired of doing it, and he was looking for any way out he could find. Jayne didn't like losing the weekend to the yard, but she also didn't like the thought of paying someone the forty or fifty dollars a month it would cost to do it.

They'd had lunch just before they started the yard work. When they finished, Jayne made some tomato soup and turkey sandwiches, and they ate and watched a nature show on P.B.S. Soc was drowsy after he ate, so as soon as he got prone on the couch, he was napping before the show ended. He slept until the news came on at six o'clock. He sat up and watched what seemed to him the same news he always saw on television: Chinese students rioting, terrorism in the Middle East, murder in the nation's Capital, civil war in Central America. When the first commercial came on, he got up and went into the bedroom and got ready to take a walk down by the cliffs to watch the sunset.

"Like to join me? Go'n'a go check out the waves," he said to Jayne as he came back into the living room.

"You're not going surfing this late, are you?" she asked.

"Naw, just looking. Wan'a go?"

"Sure. It's such a beautiful day. Bet the sunset'll be pretty."

She went into the bedroom to change, and he sat down and watched some more news. They showed some dead bodies in Beirut, and that was enough for him. He turned off the set. Then he went out onto the front porch and waited for Jayne. They walked straight down to Cowell's and from there out to the Lane. It looked like the surf might have picked up during the afternoon low tide, which wasn't really low at 1.9. There were some surfers with longboards coming up the

The Death of Soc Smith

steps at Cowell's. Soc didn't see anyone he knew. They mostly looked like Valleys, only there for the day and then back over the hill. When they walked around the point at Indicators, Soc could see that the Lane was still pumping.

"Looks like there were sets coming through all day out here," he said. "Swell's picking up. Another minus tide for dawn patrol tomorrow. I'm goin' out."

"You have fun, dear. I'm sleeping in."

When they passed where Lighthouse field started, the crowds on the bike path began to thicken. Cars in the street were lined up bumper to bumper. There was a traffic jam on both sides of the point. They found a spot on the cliff just past the parking lot at Middle Peak where they could sit down. It was a good place to watch the few remaining surfers get their last waves before the sun went down on the other side of the field.

"Boy, it seems like the traffic gets heavier every year, doesn't it?" Soc said.

"It sure isn't the same town we moved to twenty years ago," said Jayne. "It seemed like in those days the traffic was heavy on weekends and summers only. Now it's all the time."

"I wonder where it all ends, if it ends at all. Wha'da yuh think? Should we call Cary tonight and tell her about my demise?" he said, changing the subject abruptly. "Been a while since we've talked to 'er."

"Good idea. Let's call her, but we probably shouldn't say anything about the obit. or about the death certificate. It's obviously a mistake. We can tell her about it after you straighten it out. You know how emotional she gets about such things. She'll just get upset if you tell her now."

"I have a funny feeling it's not go'n'a be so easy to fix it."

"I don't see how it can't be. You're alive, and it seems to me that all you have to do is be there in person and that'll take care of it. What do you have to prove anyway? You're alive, and you know it, and I know it and everybody we know is going to know it, too. So, what else is there?"

"I don't know. I just feel funny about it, and I have a strange feeling that the county and the newspaper might not be so eager to change things."

The sun had dropped behind some cypress trees in the field across the street, casting shadows on them, and the last surfers were paddling in toward the stairs. Soc and Jayne got up and joined the throng of pedes-

The Death of Soc Smith

trians on the bike path. By the time they got around the point, the sun was halfway below the horizon and they were headed into a soft sundown west wind. They crossed the street and walked through the field on the path that brought them out in the neighborhood on the other side.

...what an incredible piece of real estate this is...it's like being in the wilderness...if you couldn't see the houses on the other side, you'd think you were out in the country, not in the middle of town...the birds are in charge here...when we first moved here, ratty old school busses were in charge out here...the field made a comeback when the cops came and rousted 'em out...while they were allowed to park here, the trees were dying and the tall grasses were matted, flat, wheel rutted...organic and synthetic human waste were everywhere...we wouldn't be able to walk where we're walking right now without stepping in someone's shit or kicking a bag of trash...they posted no camping signs a few years ago, and within days, the trees got green again...the first rainfall after the camper ban washed the dust off...the birds and squirrels and gophers came back and took over again....

The sky was dark gray as they entered the sliding door into their bedroom. They'd left a light on in the living room, which put a nice mellow glow on the setting. After they hung their jackets up, he sat down on the bed with the bedroom phone. He picked up the receiver after Jayne dialed the number in the kitchen. She called Caroline on the east coast.

"So, what're you guys up to?" she asked after they'd said their hellos.

"Not much," said Soc.

"We just got back from a walk along the cliff," Jayne said. "So, how're your classes, honey? You still getting an A in Old Testament?"

"Oh yeah. That class is fine. I'm actually having some trouble with my theology class. I only got a B on the midterm."

"You're such a perfectionist. Always have been."

"You know, there's another reason we're calling you," Soc said, not realizing the abruptness with which he'd changed the subject.

"I thought we weren't going to discuss that," Jayne said.

"We mi's well tell her," Soc said.

"What're you guys talking about?" Caroline said.

"There's something funny going on here that we won't be able to get an explana-

28

The Death of Soc Smith

tion for until Monday morning. First thing is the paper put my obituary in this morning's edition. Then your mom got a death certificate in the mail from the county office of vital statistics...."

"There's nothing to worry about," Jayne broke in. "Your father's going to go to the newspaper and the county before he goes to work on Monday, so it'll be all straightened out then."

"What?" Caroline asked, not seeking another explanation. The question was an exclamation that only expressed how shocked she was by what she'd heard.

"I'm sorry, babe," Soc said. "I didn't mean to scare you, but I just wanted to let you know what's happening and what we're doing about it. What your mom just said sums it up pretty well. I'm go'n'a take care of it on Monday."

"I'm glad you called. This is awful. Scary. I don't know what to say."

Soc felt that he could cut her anxiety with a knife, so he tried to mollify her, but he didn't think he had much success.

"Don't worry about a thing. I'll take care of it on Monday."

The conversation ended there. What else could anyone say, but the more he thought about it, the more alarming the situation became.

"Wan'a go down to the video store and get a movie?" Jayne asked after they'd hung up.

"Sure," he replied, "if I can stay awake long enough to watch it."

A half hour later they were watching *Heaven Can Wait*, with Warren Beatty playing the lead role of a football quarterback who gets hit by a car and killed while he's jogging on the highway, but he gets to stay on earth for a while longer. Jayne had no idea what it was about when she'd rented it, and she swore she wouldn't have if she had known. It wasn't exactly the thing for Soc right then, but it didn't bother him too much, as he fell asleep on the couch twenty minutes into it. Jayne lasted another twenty minutes after that, and then she turned it off and woke Soc up. The two of them walked off to the bedroom together. She was in bed and sound asleep within minutes, but somehow after he'd brushed his teeth, he couldn't get back to sleep. The events of the day still weighed heavily on his mind.

Four

Soc slept fitfully throughout the night and woke up at five-thirty. He went out to get the Sunday morning paper on the front porch. When he got back into the house, he poured himself some orange juice and fixed a bowl of cereal. Then he sat down with the newspaper and turned first to the obituaries. His heart started beating faster as he got to the page, but then it went back to normal as he was happy to see his name wasn't listed a second time. Next he turned to the weather page and looked at the tide chart. The low, at a few minutes before seven, was -1.9, even lower than yesterday.

He ate his cereal and drank his orange juice as he skimmed the front section and the sports section. He paid more attention to the comics, especially "Alley Oop," which he had to hunt for in the classified ad section. He'd first started reading the time traveler

Jerome Arthur

when he was only eleven years old and had a *Mirror News* route in Los Angeles.

...used to fold the papers 'n fronta' the eagle mart...five a.m....before sun-up...read the comics first...alley oop mandrake the magician nancy beetle bailey blondie...skimmed the front section like i do now....

He finished eating by six-fifteen, and by six-thirty he was through with the paper, too. He went out to the garage, got his surfboard down and put it in the special rack he'd fashioned inside the Woody. It was a plastic pipe framework behind the shotgun seat, which, when the board was mounted on it, allowed for adequate headroom. Soc had removed the back seat and placed a foam mat there wide enough to sleep two. He got his wetsuit and booties out of the cabinet and put them in the car. When he returned to the house, Jayne was in the kitchen toasting some frozen waffles. He hugged and kissed her and went out through the service porch door.

...go'n'a be a nice day...sky's clear... warm...hope there're waves....

And there were. Plenty of them. When he got to within a block of the cliff, he could hear their airy hissing sound through his open window. Then as he pulled out onto

The Death of Soc Smith

the cliff, he saw a set of four come rolling through all the way from Indicators. The third one in the set was the best one, and four surfers were riding it. A fifth surfer split off to the left and rode to the stairs. Even from his moving vantage point, Soc could see that it was Leonard, who took the left so much that most of the other surfers who surfed there thought he owned it. Indeed, they called that section "Leonard's Left." Three of the other surfers on the wave were friends of Soc's: Jesse, the guy he'd seen yesterday, Bart and Clint. It was a nice four-foot barrel that didn't close out till it was only about twenty feet from the beach. The fourth wave in the set never did shape up enough for anybody to catch.

Soc parked the Woody on the side street facing the cliff. He took his board out first and set it down mostly on the sidewalk, but the inside edge was just over the lawn of the house he was parked in front of. He tried to keep off the lawn as much as possible because one of these homeowners (not this one) once came out of his house and jumped all over him for putting his board on his lawn. Next he got his suit out and put it on, and then he waxed his board. When he was all ready to go out, he locked the Woody and put the key in a fob pocket in the trunks he wore under his wetsuit. He walked across the street and down the stairs to the beach.

The tide was out so far that there were a good thirty feet of beach between the steps and the water line. He set his board down in the wet sand and attached his leash. Then he walked as far out as he could along the edge of the cliff, and when he couldn't go any farther without being shin deep in water, he started heading straight out through the breaking waves. By then he was almost to Indicators. He hopped onto his board on his knees and paddled out to where the waves were peaking. Jesse, Bart and Clint had already paddled back out and were waiting for the next set. He passed Leonard waiting for his left as he headed in their direction.

"Hey, Leonard."

"Hey, Soc."

The next set started coming up as he joined the group. He was too tired from paddling out to start scrambling for the first wave in the set, so he sat on his board to rest as the first two went through. Clint caught the first one with a couple other guys; Bart paddled for the second, also a party wave. Soc had caught his breath by the time the third one was shaping up, so he started paddling for it. Jesse was right next to him going for it, too. As it curled up, he dug in hard

The Death of Soc Smith

with both arms, and he could feel it picking up the tail and pushing him toward the beach. Once he stood up, he looked over his shoulder to see that Jesse and another guy he didn't know were right behind him. He leaned a little to the right and took a couple steps forward to get into the slot. Jesse and the other guy were right with him. They rode like this for quite a while, and when the wave started to mush out, Jesse, who wasn't wearing a leash, suddenly jumped from his own board onto Soc's right behind him. They didn't ride far like this before they both fell into the water and came up laughing. The other guy had kicked out long before.

"We ought to go on the tandem circuit as a team," Jesse said.

"Yeah," Soc said. "What a ride that was!"

Now he had to paddle all the way back out. This was the part of surfing that made him think he might be getting too old for it. He found himself stopping and resting several times before he got back out to the lineup. Jesse, who was a few years younger than Soc, paddled straight back out without stopping. He passed Clint who was already riding another inside wave.

...look at this...another inside wave...can i catch it?...i'm really

pooped...perfect   spot...just   get   turned around here....

He turned around and got right into the slot, and as tired as he was, he started paddling, but he just didn't have enough momentum to catch it, and so it rolled right under him and started breaking about ten feet beyond. Now he was really out of breath, so he turned around and started paddling slowly back out to the lineup. Clint hadn't gone far on the wave, so he was right next to Soc paddling back out, too.

"Great day, huh, Soc?" Clint said as they both rested after only a few strokes.

"So far, so good," Soc gasped. "I just got in the water and already got a couple rides."

"I only got in a little while ago my-self, and I haven't missed a set. You see Bart and Jesse?"

"Yeah, Jesse and I were just riding the same wave. Didn't you see us do our tan-dem thing?"

"Nah, I missed that one."

They continued paddling out. There was a break. No sets coming through. When they got back to the lineup, Bart and Jesse were already there, sitting on their boards waiting for waves. There were maybe twenty surfers in the water, not very crowded for a

The Death of Soc Smith

Sunday. And it was turning into a pretty day, beautiful sunrise. They waited, fifteen minutes for another set. At one point Clint, facing the horizon, raised his arms in supplication to the great god of the surf, praying for more waves. He'd do this in jest to break the monotony of waiting for the waves, and of course, the waves started coming almost as soon as he did it.

Soc stayed in the water for a good three hours. As the tide came in, the sets were fewer and further between. By ten o'clock it was flattening out, and it had started getting crowded an hour before that. There were now fifty or more surfers in the water. The Valleys were out in full force. He'd caught more than his share of waves, so many that he'd lost count a couple hours ago. It had been a good day in one other important respect: no one had said anything about his demise. Either they didn't read the newspaper or they read it and missed the obituary. Whichever, he didn't care. He was just glad that nobody had said anything about it. He'd forgotten about it himself the whole time he was in the water.

After about a twenty-minute wait, he saw a set of small waves start to come through. He managed to catch the first one, which was only about a foot high, and he rode it left all the way into the steps. It was so small that he didn't even try to stand up. He got up to his knees and paddled with both arms, riding mostly white water until he was in knee-deep water. He got off his board and undid his leash and started up the steps.

He huffed and puffed his way to the top of the stairs and over to his Woody. He was so beat, it took him twenty minutes to get his suit off and get his board back into the car. When he finished, he walked back over to the cliff and sat down to rest and watch the last remaining Valleys trying to catch waves in the diminishing sets. The other guys had gone home already, so after a few minutes, Soc got up and went to his car and did the same.

Five

He pulled the Woody into the garage, dragged himself out and opened the tailgate to unload his surfing gear. He took the wetsuit and surfboard out the side door to the patio that separated the garage from the house. He hosed them down, stood the board up against the side of the garage, and hung the suit on a wooden hanger from a hook screwed into the wall. He rinsed off under the outdoor shower on the back wall of the house. The patio was completely enclosed and private with six-foot high redwood fences that ran from the house to the garage.

He stepped into the house through the sliding door to his bedroom and started to get dressed. Jayne came through the other door telling him that she had lunch for him.

At the dining room table, Jayne finally mentioned the county death certificate. They hadn't talked about it much since it arrived, unconsciously maintaining an attitude that it wouldn't exist if you didn't talk about it.

"So, what are you going to do about this business with the death certificate?" she asked.

"Same thing I'm go'n'a do about the obit. in the paper. Go'n'a show up in person, show 'em my driver's license and birth certificate. It's just a clerical error. Go'n'a try to get the paper to print a retraction. What else *can* I do?"

Even though he thought what he was saying was the logical thing to happen, he wasn't sure he believed it would.

"I'm worried. First the newspaper article, and now this thing with the county. It all just seems so official and final. Something's going on, and I don't know what it is."

"Same thought's occurred to me, but right now, I don't know what else to do but go talk to 'em, try to get it undone."

He didn't think about the significance of the word "try" at that moment. He could only wonder what it's importance would be in the next few days.

They dropped the subject. Soc went into the living room and turned the television on to *Wide World of Sports*, but he didn't stick with it long. He was hoping to see some

The Death of Soc Smith

surfing, but they rarely ever showed any surfing on that program. They were doing golf, and, even though he wasn't averse to playing a round or two himself, he couldn't think of anything more boring than watching some other guys playing the game.

He changed the channel to a boxing match. He watched a round until a commercial came on. He jumped around the channels for a couple minutes and then he switched back to the fight. He watched that round, and then he turned the T.V. off and went out to the patio to check to see if his board was dry. It was, but the suit needed to hang a while longer. He put the board away and went back out onto the patio and sat down in a chaise lounge in the shade. Within minutes he was sound asleep. He stayed that way until late afternoon.

While he slept, he had a dream. There were no details in the dream leading up to the announcement by his family doctor that he, Soc, was suffering from some incurable terminal disease, and he had only a few weeks to live. Soc's initial reaction in the dream was denial.

…this isn't happening to me….

The real Soc lying there sleeping on the patio was scared shitless, and his heart was pounding in his chest. In the dream he

41

made the rational decision that he wasn't going to suffer. He would get on his surfboard without a wetsuit and paddle out to sea. He knew if sharks didn't get him, like they got that guy up the coast a while back, then mother ocean would, and that's how he wanted to go anyway, not in a hospital, plugged up to space age machinery whose only function, it seemed to Soc, was to keep dead people alive no matter how much they suffered. Well, he needn't have worried about any of it. As he was heading toward the beach, shivering in his trunks, surfboard under his arm, he suddenly woke up, but he was by no means calm and feeling rested. His heart was pounding wildly.

He got to his feet and tried to orient himself, paced around and thought about the dream, never thought of doing what he'd started to do in the dream. If he were ever to come down with a crippling or terminal disease, at that moment he thought it might not be such a bad idea. He'd rather die on his surfboard in the ocean than go through prolonged suffering. He took his wetsuit off the hook on the outside of the garage and hung it on one of the dowels that held the board.

When he went into the house, he discovered he was alone. Jayne had gone somewhere. He sat down on the couch and

The Death of Soc Smith

turned on the television. "The McLaughlin Group" came up on the screen. The panel was debating whether more members of congress would be resigning because of recent ethics scandals. When the show ended, Soc turned the T.V. off. He put on some grubby clothes and headed out to the garage. The sun was still in the sky, plenty of light, so he thought he'd tinker with the Woody. He raised the garage door and reached inside the car to release the hand brake. He pushed it out onto the driveway apron. It was all level concrete, so it wasn't hard to do. He didn't want to fire it up for the two minutes it would take to move it. He lifted the heavy old hood of the car.

...damn sure don't make 'em like they used to...hood on jayne's car's like tinfoil compared to this...look at this engine...big, solid, and only a six, like jayne's, only bigger and more powerful....

He looked in at the engine, checked the oil. It was good, right in between the two lines, closer to the top line. When he checked the radiator, he could see the upper hose needed to be replaced.

...just something else to add to the list of things to do tomorrow...get a radiator hose at andy's...might be needing this car

ready to go anywhere, anytime…hell, who knows?…i might be dead after all….

The water level was up, so it wasn't leaking yet, but it looked like it could start any minute. He didn't take the hose off, but instead made a note to buy a new one and put it in when he got home from work tomorrow afternoon. He lowered the hood and put his butt on the rear bumper and pushed the car back in. He closed the garage door from inside and exited through the side door. As he crossed the patio to the house, he heard Jayne's car pull up onto the apron.

He stood and waited for her to come through the gate. She carried a flat brown paper bag with a downtown shop logo printed on it. When she got to him, he put his arm around her shoulder, and they walked side by side through the slider into the house.

"Where'd you go?" he asked.

"Went to the gift shop on the Mall and bought some thank you cards for the volunteer aides who have been in my class all semester."

When they got to the dining room table, she took them out of the bag and showed them to him. She tried to get him to read them and then she'd explain each one to him, but he only looked at them absently, not paying too much attention to what she said. He

The Death of Soc Smith

was clearly distracted. He had other things on his mind. But then so did she. She was only chattering on like this as a diversion from what was really on her mind.

Her school year was coming to an end, and as always, she was enthusiastic about the coming of summer and its ten weeks of "down time." It was different this year, though. True, during the next month she'd be going to various end-of-the-year parties, giving and receiving presents, and saying goodbye to those who wouldn't be returning in the fall. And when it was over, she'd settle into working on her summer home improvement projects, which always included something for Soc to do. That's what she'd always done in the past, but now things had changed. She was off her game. She had always been so steady and consistent; now she felt scattered and conflicted.

"Wha'da yuh say we go out to dinner?" Soc said.

"Sure, where you wan'a go?" She was glad he'd interrupted her negative thoughts.

"How 'bout someplace out on the Wharf? I feel like seafood."

"'Sounds good. What time?"

"Let's make it six o'clock."

"I'll be ready."

"Maybe we could stop at the video store on the way home and rent a movie."

"Sure. 'Sounds like a plan. Just let me put this stuff away and feed the cats, and we can go."

While she was doing that, Soc went into the bedroom and changed clothes. When Jayne finished her chore, she put on some lipstick. They went out the back door and crossed the patio to the car. She got in the driver's seat; Soc rode shotgun.

Six

By seven-fifteen they were seated at their table overlooking Cowell's Cove where he'd surfed that morning. The sun was descending to the rooftops of the houses that lined the cliff across the water. It would be sinking behind them within half an hour. The lighthouse, backlit by the sunset, looked like a blue/gray silhouette drawn against the soon-to-be-darkening sky. The surfers at the Lane looked like ants from that distance. Three sailboats were making their way back toward the harbor mouth, their sails tattooed to the line of the horizon that separated the still light blue sky from the blue/green ocean.

"Tomorrow while you're running around trying to prove you're alive, I'll be busy doing my end-of-year routine with the kids. I've got one I'll be holding back."

"Ooh, that's tough. Parents not happy about that?"

"They usually aren't."

"'Sounds like a rough day."

"It will be. The parents usually don't want to hold their kids back. These ones have been pretty good at the parent conferences, so maybe they'll think holding the boy back is a good idea. I think it'll be the best thing for him."

The waitress took their order, and when she left, they fell silent and watched the sun sink next to the Dream Inn, the seven-story motel overlooking Cowell's Beach. Cars, looking like little toys from this distance, crept along the cliff.

...seen this scene from every angle in the last couple days...yesterday morning from up on the cliff looking this way...today from in the water...now on the other side looking back...all in the point of view....

The restaurant was crowded when they got there. They'd waited ten minutes to get seated by the window. Now the crowd was thinning out.

Because the service was good, they got out of there before dark. He bought them a couple cups of gelato and followed her out of the restaurant. It was a warm evening, so they took a stroll on the wharf. They didn't go far before crossing to the other side and starting back. The Boardwalk was closed, and as the sky got darker, the roller coaster

The Death of Soc Smith

and Ferris wheel looked like gigantic skeletons on the eastern horizon. The beach was almost deserted by now. The weekenders were gone, thus leaving it to a few locals who were taking their evening walks. Soc and Jayne got into the car and drove off the wharf and headed to the video store. Soc went to the classics section of the store and picked up a copy of *Casablanca*. Then he went over to where Jayne was looking at some more contemporary titles.

"Wha'cha got?" she said.

"*Casablanca*. How about you?"

"I'm thinking about *Lethal Weapon*. Mel Gibson and Danny Glover. I remember liking it when we saw it in the movie theater."

"'Sounds good. Go ahead and get it. I'll put this one back."

He met her at the counter after he took *Casablanca* back. When they got home, Jayne fixed up some lemonade and popcorn, and Soc moved the pillows on the couch. He set the tape up in the V.C.R. and fast-forwarded it past the trailers of future releases on video and the F.B.I. warning. She wasn't quite finished in the kitchen, so he went into the bedroom, took off his trousers and put on a pair of sweatpants. Back in the living room, Jayne was setting the snacks on the coffee table. She went into the bedroom and changed into her nightgown and terry cloth robe.

They both stayed awake, watching the movie all the way through. Of course, Soc knew that most of Jayne's interest in watching it was to see Mel Gibson. He was what she called a "hunk." But she would also claim that she liked other things about the movie too, like the story. When it was over, they cleaned up the mess they'd made and got ready for bed.

"I'll drop the video off on my way to the county building tomorrow morning," Soc said. "I'm go'n'a try to be there by eight when they open. They are open then, aren't they? Or is it nine?"

"Hmm. I really don't know. I've never gone there first thing in the morning. I'm sure it must be eight."

"That's when I'll go. I won't even plan on going to work until after lunch."

They read for a few minutes after they got in bed. He was still working on *The Lady in the Lake*. She was reading something in *The New Yorker*. It was now late, and they didn't read for long. First Jayne dropped her magazine on the floor next to her side of the bed, and shortly after that Soc set his book

The Death of Soc Smith

down and turned out the lamp on the nightstand.

Seven

Soc didn't sleep much that night. He was thinking about what he would say to the people at the newspaper and the county, rehearsing it over and over again in his mind. He finally fell asleep at ten-thirty and awoke at three in the morning to go to the bathroom. When he got back into bed, he stared at the ceiling until four. When he finally did doze off again, he had a dream in which he went to all the places he was going to in the morning, but all the people he dealt with didn't even acknowledge his existence. He was invisible, shouting at people trying to convince them that he was alive and present, but it was all to no avail. He was pretty exhausted when he woke up. It was only five-thirty, but he was wide awake and couldn't go back to sleep now if his life depended on it, so he got out of bed, pulled on his loungers and went out to get the morning paper.

The Death of Soc Smith

Monday's paper was thin as usual, so it didn't take him long to go through it. He'd read everything that interested him by six o'clock and was glad to see that his name didn't appear on the obituary page.

...of course...why would it?...they wouldn't publish an obituary twice...and it wasn't there yesterday...so what's the big deal....

He toasted a couple of Eggo waffles and put a bottle of syrup in a saucepan to boil on the stove. He ate and then washed the dishes. By then Jayne was in the kitchen too, feeding the cats. They exchanged good mornings, and he told her about his dream, but he realized afterward that he shouldn't have. It only amplified her feelings of insecurity, and Soc watched the gloomy veil of uncertainty fall over her face. After some half-hearted reassurances, he moved off toward the patio to take his shower as she began making herself something for breakfast and packing a brown bag for lunch.

Soc was dressed and ready by seven o'clock. It was about an hour before low tide, which was going to be minus one point six. He thought he'd go look. He had plenty of time. Jayne wouldn't be leaving for work until a quarter to eight. He figured he could go check out the waves and get back in time to kiss her goodbye before Betty, her carpool partner, came to pick her up. So, he went into the kitchen where she was still fretting over his dream and washing her breakfast dishes. He told her his plan and left by the back door, walking across the patio to the garage.

Being behind the wheel of the Woody was always a comfort to him. It was a forty-eight Chevy, very similar to his first car, which was the same year and make, but a different model. The model he had back then was the Aero Sedan, or "Torpedo Back" as he, his dad, and just about everybody else he knew, called it at the time. He first saw the Woody when he was forty-seven years old, and he was so filled with nostalgia when he looked in the driver side window and saw that old familiar dashboard and steering wheel. He knew right then and there that he had to have the car. It had a "FOR SALE" sign in the window, so he took down the number and called about it later. When he sat behind the wheel, his teenage memories flooded in on him. It was at that moment that he made up his mind to buy it. He was sold on it before he even took it for a test hop.

Now he was cruising down to the cliffs, and the car was a comfort to him. With all the turmoil of his "death" going on, the car was his only true sanctuary. He zig

The Death of Soc Smith

zagged through the neighborhood, coming out on the cliff at the stairs.

He pulled over and parked as close to the corner as he could get. As he walked over to the cliff, he couldn't see Jesse's car anywhere.

...monday...he's at work....

Bart's and Clint's trucks were in the parking spaces next to the cliff. They were in the water along with about twenty other surfers; Leonard was just getting into his suit. Soc could see the sets coming through as he got closer. The waves were waist to chest high; there were three waves in the set he was looking at. He walked over and talked to Leonard as he waxed his board.

"Looks like some pretty good sets comin' through," said Soc. "Been goin' on for a while?"

"Yeah. Been watching for about a half hour, and it's been consistent. Bart and Clint just went out. They've each gotten a couple waves already. Left just started breaking good right now."

"I wish I could go out."

"Why don't you?"

"Aw, I've got some business to take care of. Maybe if I get done early enough, I can come back."

It was the first he'd thought of surfing as an option for the day's activity.

...why not?...could take the day off after i get this death stuff taken care of...haven't taken a sick day in a long time, and god knows i got plenty of 'em comin'...can't remember the last time i went surfing on a week day...c'n claim i'm celebrating bein' alive....

Leonard picked up his board and started for the stairs. Soc turned and went back to the Woody and got in. On his way back home, he took the scenic route around the point where the waves were well overhead and there were plenty of guys out.

Back at the house, Jayne was putting on her makeup as *The Today Show* blared out of the television set in the other room. He sat down and watched Jane Pauley interview Woody Allen. At twenty to eight Betty honked her horn out front, and Jayne came out of the bedroom with her tote bag full of goodies for the day. She hugged and kissed Soc and told him to call her as soon as he got things cleared up. Then she was gone.

Soc turned the television off and suddenly the house seemed so quiet and deserted. He shuddered and felt an urgency to get out of there. He picked up the telephone and

The Death of Soc Smith

called work to let them know what was happening and that he'd be late getting there.

"I...I'm sorry Mister Smith," the voice at the other end stammered, "but...could you hold for a moment?" And before he could respond, he was put on hold.

"Hello, Mister Smith," a voice said after what seemed like an hour but was really only a minute. "This is Jim Jones from personnel. There must be some mistake here. I was informed late Friday that you had passed away, and therefore would no longer be employed here. So, I spent Saturday, my day off, interviewing applicants for the vacat-ed position. By three o'clock, someone was hired, and he just reported for work five minutes ago. He's working at your desk right now. I'm not quite sure what to do."

"Well, you can start by firing my replacement because I'll be there in about an hour, and I expect to sit down at my desk and go to work. In the meantime, I'm going to the county building and the newspaper to get things straightened out at their end. Obviously, I'm not dead, and I do need my job because I have responsibilities which will require my having a steady paycheck."

"I'm sorry Mister Smith, but I don't think I can do that. Perhaps if I connected you with Mister Johmstock, the vice president in charge management/personnel liaison."

"I don't think so. I'll talk to him in person when I get there."

And he hung up.

...i don't believe this...gets curiouser and curiouser to quote casey stengel, or was that yogi berra?...the hell's goin' on here?...i'm sure glad jayne didn't hear this conversation...i can just see myself tryin' to explain it to her...she'd be pretty upset, and that wouldn't do anybody any good, least of all me...trying to deal with the bureaucrats is go'n'a be hard enough...i ain't go'n'a have time to be worrying about whether she's go'n'a be okay....

He left the house, glad to be out of its quiet, deserted confines. With no one there but him and the cats, the place was as still as the desert at high noon in July. Jayne and Betty alternated days driving, so Soc had the family car to run his ghoulish errands. Usually he'd walk to the corner and take the bus to work on Jayne's driving days.

He got to the county building by eight-ten, but he couldn't find a parking place in the parking lot, so he crossed the boulevard that went to the beach and parked in the neighborhood behind Jack in the Box. It was just one more thing working against him, one more obstacle to overcome on a day that would be filled with stumbling blocks.

...probably trip on the stairs going into the damn county building....

The county building was a five-story concrete box, which Soc referred to as the five-story basement. He never could figure how something so ugly and unaesthetic could possibly be built. He went to the directory and found the office he was looking for on the second floor. He took the steps. Entering the office, he was confronted by a long counter, behind which stood a dour looking woman whose gray hair matched her concrete gray cheeks and brow, and these blended with the decor and the architecture.

"May I help you, sir?" she asked. Her voice was just as stern as her appearance.

"I sure hope so," Soc said, screwing up his resolve. "There must be some mistake here."

He laid the death certificate on the counter in front of her. Reaching for his wallet with his other hand, he took his driver's license out and set it down next to the document.

"Yes?" the woman said and gave him a look like she didn't understand what his problem was.

"Well, you'll note the name here says, 'Socrates Smith.' Same name as my driver's license here. I've got news for you. I'm not dead. I'm Socrates Smith, and I'd like to get this undone, because as you can see, I'm very much alive."

"Oh," was her only reply, and then with knitted brow, she studied the document and the license. After a few minutes, she looked up at him and said, "Can you prove you're Socrates Smith?"

He couldn't believe the question.

"Look at the picture on the license. I can bring in the lady you sent this certificate to. It's my wife Jayne, and she can verify my identity and tell you I'm not dead."

As he was talking, a cement gray man walked out from the back and up to the counter. He peered over the woman's shoulder at the death certificate, making no comment.

"We do have a problem here, don't we?" the woman said when she'd finished looking at the document. "However, I'm not sure there's anything we can do about it. Once these things are issued, they can't be nullified. You can take it up with our department head, but I don't think it'll do any good. He has no more power or authority than I do to abrogate this."

The Death of Soc Smith

Her sternness was intimidating, but Soc was undaunted. The man next to her was completely obtuse. He merely stood by with a vacuous expression on his face.

"I can't believe what you're telling me," said Soc. "What you're saying basically is that I'm dead, no matter how obviously alive I am, and furthermore, there's nobody who can change this. And the only person who can fix it won't be able to help me out here. He's just go'n'a declare me dead, too. Now that's ridiculous."

"What difference does it make?" she said. "You're alive, and you know it, so why don't you just go about your business and be alive. This is only a piece of paper, and it doesn't really signify anything."

Soc looked at the man and only saw an empty grin on his face, which only increased his frustration with the situation.

"Who exactly requested this death certificate, anyway?" Soc asked.

"I'm sorry, sir, but I'm not authorized to give out that information to anyone except the next of kin to the deceased, and then only by special request. Our primary concern in cases like this is to protect the identity of the person or persons who requested it."

"I don't believe this. It sounds like just about anybody can request a death certificate be filed on anybody else, no questions asked, and then the requesting person's identity is protected, even if he did it erroneously or as a practical joke."

"You're simplifying the situation somewhat. Not just anybody can request a death certificate. Usually it's someone in some official capacity, like the coroner, for example, and the requests are usually justified. Now, what I suggest, Mister Smith, is that you talk to the director of vital statistics, and then perhaps you'll determine how one was issued on you, although it's very possible nothing will be resolved."

In a daze Soc turned away from the counter and started toward the door. Then he turned back, walked up to the counter and asked the cement lady what he had to do to talk to the director of vital statistics.

Eight

After an hour of wrangling around with various county bureaucrats, including the director of vital statistics, and getting no satisfaction, Soc walked back to his car more exhausted than he'd been when he awoke after his bizarre dream. He was worn down like when he was in the Navy and he'd been dealing with these types all day long every day for the three years of his hitch. Once he'd been pulled off his regular duties to work on reports for a plane crash that killed eight men. When commander Powers, the officer he reported to, told him that he'd be working temporarily under his command, he also told Soc that he'd be relieved of all his other duties. So, when Soc's duty night came, he didn't report for muster with the duty section, and he'd been scheduled to stand a mid watch. The next day commander Powers informed him that he was on report for missing his watch. When Soc tried to remind him that he'd been told his only duty was to work on the crash reports, he was rebuked soundly, and commander Powers told him that he, Powers, was not authorized to exempt him from the duty section. That was one incident; there'd been hundreds of others.

The lady with the concrete face behind the counter had used the same words—"not authorized"—to get out of solving Soc's problem. The other people he'd talked to at the county used them, too. All of them had taken out rulebooks and used them as shields against further inquiry from Soc, which really confused and frustrated him. He didn't know quite where to go from there. It was just as it had been in the dream. He was talking, but nobody could hear him, and in fact his encounters in those offices had the quality of unreality that exists only in dreams. The dialogue was circular, and it always came back to where Soc was dead, and there was nothing anybody could do to revive him, least of all anybody in the county offices.

He was talking to himself as he crossed the parking lot on the way to his car. He didn't notice the people looking at him the way they looked at the dropouts from county mental health who hung around the downtown mall behaving badly. At that moment it would have been difficult to tell the difference between them and Soc by the way he was acting.

...how can they be so oblivious?...this is bullshit...i really don't give a damn what their records say...it just pisses me off they can stand there and not see how stupid something is and make the changes so it's not stupid anymore....

When he got to his car, there was a ticket under the windshield wiper. He was parked in a one-hour zone, and he'd been gone an hour and twenty minutes.

...damn meter maid must've watched me park...is this go'n'a be my day, or what?...

He unlocked the door and got in behind the wheel. He threw the ticket onto the seat next to him. Then he started the car and crossed the river back into downtown to the newspaper office.

He pulled into the first parking space he came to. Luckily, it was still early enough in the morning and there were many parking places to choose from. He grabbed one that was by itself with a driveway at the rear of the car and a street corner at the front. It had a parking meter, so he had to go into the coffee shop he was parked in front of and buy a pint of orange juice for a dollar and a quarter to get some change. He got one hour, which was the maximum on this meter, for two quarters. He was parked about halfway between the auto supply and the newspaper.

He got the radiator hose at the auto supply and took it back to the car. He put another dime in the meter on his way to the newspaper, and that put it back up to an hour. He didn't want to get another ticket, and he really didn't want to spend that much time talking to the editor.

"What a terrible thing to happen," the woman behind the counter said as Soc showed her the obituary from Saturday's paper and explained to her who he was. "I'm sure we can get this taken care of."

Then she got on the phone and was talking to someone who could presumably solve the problem. When she hung up, she told him to go up the stairs and down the hall to the last door on the right where he would find the editor's office.

"He's expecting you," she said, "and he'll fix it for you."

The newsroom was at the top of the stairs, but Soc walked right past it and down the hall to the editor's office. He knocked on the door and a voice from within beckoned him to enter. When he did, he was in an office that had a window wall with open blinds

The Death of Soc Smith

facing the newsroom, and as he closed the door behind him, the man behind the desk stood up and walked over to shut the blinds, thus giving the office privacy from the newsroom.

"Now, what seems to be the trouble here?" asked the editor, whose nameplate on his desk identified him as James Jacobs. "Am I to understand that we published a death notice on you, and you're not dead?"

"That's about it in a nutshell," Soc said. "And I'm not just here to inform you of the mistake. I also want a retraction."

Jacobs merely leaned back in his chair, elbows resting on the chair arms with his hands folded in front of him, his chin perched on his thumbs, his forefingers pointing up and pressed against his lips. It was a good three minutes before he spoke. He seemed to be contemplating the situation, but for some reason, he didn't appear to Soc to be perceptive enough for any kind of deep thought. When he started talking, Soc knew he'd pegged him right.

"You know, this is a crazy spot you're in here. I honestly don't know what we can do about it. I don't think you realize how difficult a job it is trying to run this newsroom. Take a look at this."

He slid a piece of paper across his desk to Soc. It was a letter with all the information concerning Soc's death. No signature, no letterhead or return address, but otherwise very official looking.

"You see, we get these all the time, and of course we have to act on them when they come in. I even have to sign for them before they can be opened. So, as you can see, it's all very official, and these things can't be taken lightly."

He got up from his desk and walked over to the window wall and opened the blinds and stared out into the newsroom.

"I think what you need to do before we can do anything, Mister Smith, is go to the post office to find out the source of this letter. Once you've done that, you'll need a notarized statement from that source indicating that it is a mistake. Then I think we can do something for you. Until you do all those things, we cannot be of assistance to you."

"Yeah, I know, don't tell me. You're not authorized to do anything here."

"That is exactly correct, Mister Smith."

"Not the first time I've heard that line. What is this nonsense? Here I am. Alive. Warm flesh. Blood flowing through

The Death of Soc Smith

my veins and arteries, and here's my I.D. to boot. Quite frankly, I think you can take care of this right now. And I think you should."

"I'm afraid not, Mister Smith. If you like, I could get you an appointment with our publisher, who is also vice president in charge of all editorial decisions of this newspaper."

Soc barely heard the last words trailing off behind him as he left Jacobs' office. He went through the hall to the stairway and descended to the main floor where the woman behind the counter by the door smiled at him as he exited the building. He went back to his car. The meter still had ten minutes left on it.

Nine

He drove out to the highway and headed toward the office. It was past rush hour, so the traffic was pretty light. Just before he got to where the two highways split and merged, he saw a pretty bad accident up ahead. A B.M.W. was in the lane that went to the right onto Highway 1 south, when it suddenly and without warning veered left to go north on Highway 17. There was a Volvo station wagon in that lane going south, and the B.M.W. cut him off. The wagon glanced off the concrete merge barrier where the two freeways split and came to stop at the end of the divider. Soc was about a quarter of a mile behind this scene, and he watched as the B.M.W. sped away. As he got closer to the Volvo, he could see a bloody hand waving out the driver's side window. He pulled up and stopped to see if he could be of any help.

The Death of Soc Smith

As he got out of his car and walked to the Volvo, he could see a highway patrol car approaching. When he got to the wrecked car, he looked in the open window and saw that the driver had a bloody nose, but he was conscious, and really was more shaken than hurt. His seat belt was buckled, so he was pretty much intact. The car hadn't struck the wall head-on, so the engine compartment wasn't completely squashed, just the driver's side where the front fender was totaled. The highway patrolman was talking into his microphone as he pulled up.

"You see what happened?" he asked Soc when he got out of his car and approached the bleeding man.

"I's about a quarter mile back when it happened," Soc replied. "A green B.M.W. cut the poor guy off, and then took off up the freeway. Too far away to get a license number. Maybe you'd better look at this guy."

The officer walked up to the Volvo and asked the driver how he was doing. He was conscious, but he was really dazed and unable to speak coherently. The officer told him to put his head back and try to relax. An ambulance was on the way. Then he turned his attention back to Soc.

"What exactly did you see?" the officer asked.

He jotted down the details as Soc told him what he'd seen. In the distance a siren was getting louder as it got closer.

"Did the B.M.W. signal for a lane change, or did he just pull into this guy's lane?"

"No signal. I was too far away to see, but I don't even think the guy looked over his shoulder to see if the lane was occupied. He just pulled over."

"And what's your name, sir?"

Soc got out his driver's license and gave it to the policeman. After the officer copied down the information, he said he could go, and as he was getting back into his car to continue on his way to work, an ambulance pulled up. He started up his car, and looking into his side and rear-view mirrors, he saw a tow truck coming down the freeway. He pulled out onto the highway and again was on his way to his office. The rest of the trip was without incident. He turned at his off-ramp and doubled back along the frontage road to work. He had an assigned parking space in the company lot, and when he tried to pull into it, he couldn't, because a car was already parked there. He drove around the lot and pulled into a visitor's parking space with only a half hour limit. He crossed the parking lot and entered the build-

The Death of Soc Smith

ing by the front door. He usually went in through a door at the side of the building. As he was walking past the receptionist, she looked at him as though she were seeing a ghost.

"Mister Smith!" she said, "I thought you...."

"I know. You thought I was dead. Well, so do some other people, but I've got news for all of you. The final score isn't in yet. Is Josh in his office?"

"Yes, he is, but he's in a meeting."

He ignored her, walking right past her and down the hall to his boss's office. Instead of going in, he decided to go to his own office and check things out there. On his way there one of his co-workers came out of the men's room, and when he saw Soc, his mouth dropped open and he looked at him the same way the receptionist had. Soc didn't stop to talk to him, but instead continued on to his office.

When he got there, he didn't knock or hesitate; he went right in. The door wouldn't open all the way because there was a packing box behind it. Passing through the door, he was confronted by a man about twenty years younger than he, sitting at his desk with all the drawers pulled open, and he was clearly cleaning them out. The young man, like the others, turned pale and his mouth dropped open when he saw Soc. He looked over at the packed box with the picture of Soc, Jayne and Caroline on top. It was stacked neatly on top of two other pictures, one of Jayne, the other of Caroline. Then he looked up again at Soc, and his color went from white to red. He was obviously embarrassed for having packed up Soc's personal things and was taken completely by surprise by his appearance. Soc didn't say a word to him. He turned around immediately and headed back to Josh Miller's office.

He didn't knock on Josh's door either. He stepped right in and found Josh in a meeting with the production manager. Both men fell silent when they saw him.

"My god, Soc, what's going on here?" Josh finally asked after this moment of silence.

"I don't know. You tell me. Who the hell's the kid who's cleaning out my desk?"

"Something is definitely wrong here. I'm…I don't quite know what to say. I was told on Saturday morning that you'd died. This morning when you called was the first I heard otherwise. I helped Jones select and interview the kid in your office. I don't know what the hell's going on here."

The Death of Soc Smith

"Maybe you ought'a try to figure it out. Start by going upstairs and having a talk with the boss and see if we can find out how the hell all this happened. Look, Josh, I've been all over the place this morning trying, with zero luck, to prove that I'm alive, and what do I have to prove anyway? Here I am. Wan'a fingerprint me?"

The production manager, Gillis, sat on the soft leather couch opposite the desk, and all he could do was stare at Soc in disbelief.

"What are you doing here, Smith?" he finally asked. "I heard you died."

Gillis was a sixty-year-old native of the area whom Soc saw occasionally (very occasionally, the last time maybe six months ago) in the lineup out at Cowell's when low tides got into harmony with big south swells. He grew up surfing all the spots along this coast, but now if he went out once a year, he was lucky. Soc hoped that never happened to *him*. He ignored Gillis' comment and kept staring at Josh.

"Well, I guess we should go on up and talk to Jones in personnel, find out if he knows anything more'n me."

Josh was being judicious. He was really embarrassed because he hadn't checked it out and found out if Soc's death was real or not. So now he had to go straighten it out with the personnel manager, and that wasn't going to be easy. Jones was difficult even when the problem wasn't complicated. Josh straightened up his tie and put on his suit jacket.

Soc followed him out of the office and to the elevator, which they took to the third floor. Stepping out of the elevator, they moved toward Jones's office. This floor, being where the head of the company also had his office, was much more plush and luxurious than the floor where Soc's and Josh's offices were. Plush gray, wall-to-wall carpet spread out around them, silencing their footsteps.

"We'd like to talk to Mister Jones," Josh said to the receptionist. She picked up the handset and pressed a button on her phone,

"Mister Miller and Mister Smith to see you, sir."

She paused to hear his response, after which she put the handset back in its cradle and said to Soc and Josh,

"Have a seat. He'll be right with you."

They took seats on the leather couch along the wall. Josh didn't ask Soc any questions, and Soc had no answers to supply, so

The Death of Soc Smith

they simply sat in silence waiting for Jones to come out and invite them into his office. Five minutes passed, and Jones opened the door to his office and exited with someone neither of them recognized.

"We'll take care of it before the end of the day," he said as they shook hands. The man moved off to the elevators and Jones came over and shook hands with the two men as they stood up. He smiled and said, "Hello, Josh, Soc. Come on into my office."

A window wall behind Jones's desk showed a sweeping view of the valley below, the only flaw being the ribbon of freeway and its cars racing in both directions.

"Be seated," Jones said as he took his seat in the leather chair behind his desk. "Looks like we have a bit of a problem here." This after they'd sat in the two chairs facing the desk.

"Well," Josh began. "It seems someone's made a terrible mistake, and you may be the only one that can fix it. You see, Soc here has somehow gotten himself declared dead, and as you can plainly see, he's very much alive. His job's already been filled. As you know, we hired this young man, Sneely."

"Ah, yes, Saturday it was. Fine young fellow. We spirited him away from I.B.M. So, what is it you want me to do?"

"Well, Jim, as you can plainly see, Soc here didn't die, and he's still got a few years to go before he qualifies for retirement, but this Sneely fellow's already set up in his office."

"Of course. And that's where he'll stay, too. We have another position for Smith here. It's a promotion to a different department. Small increase in salary." This to Soc. Now back to Josh. "We want to keep Sneely in Smith's old job. The position was one of the lures we used to get him here. Now, Smith, you can take the rest of the week off with pay with no vacation time deducted, and on Monday you'll report to Gillis in production. He'll show you what you'll be doing over there."

"Begging your pardon," Soc said, "but I don't have any experience in production; I'll be lost over there. I was educated and trained for my old job, and I've been doing it for almost twenty years."

He didn't say it out loud to them, but he felt sure they were trying to ease him out of the company.

"I know, I know, but sometimes we have to make these adjustments for the good of the company. That you've been doing the same job for twenty years is precisely why we want you to move over to production. I'm sure you'll do quite all right in your new position, and as for Sneely doing your job, I'm sure you'll find him quite qualified to handle it. We have high hopes for that boy in this company."

Soc was nonplussed by Jones's comments. He had the sickening feeling that they were trying to get rid of him. He had the distinct impression that they'd already planned to move him out before his death notice, and now they were merely using the bogus obituary as justification for his removal. He looked at Josh, who only shrugged his shoulders, and offered no support.

"Now, if you have no further questions," Jones continued, "we'll terminate this meeting now, and you can report to Gillis next Monday morning."

Soc had a lot of questions, but he was feeling powerless to ask them. He felt like he was left hanging out to dry. Case closed. No debate.

Ten

Confused and agitated were the only words that could adequately express Soc's feelings as he rode the elevator back down to Josh's office. The morning had slipped by quickly. Soc felt that time was running out.

Josh offered to take Soc out to lunch, but he turned him down. He needed something to relieve the tension he was feeling in his neck and shoulders, and it certainly wasn't going to be found anywhere around the plant. What he needed was to go surfing, and he was going to be able to do that for the rest of the week. There was already a knot in his guts when he got there. Now it felt like a twenty-pound boulder. Nothing had been resolved. They still didn't acknowledge the fact that Soc hadn't died.

Josh was the last person he wanted to be with just then. His silent shrug up in Jones's office was a clear signal to Soc that Josh didn't care if he was dead or alive, or whether he had a job or not. It was like he shrugged Soc off. He was developing a strong aversion to these surroundings and these people he'd worked with for so many years, and he couldn't tell if he'd been feeling that way all along, or if it was just now when he saw their true colors. And the big question was, why hadn't he seen their true colors until now?

Since everything seemed to be all arranged, and there wasn't much he could do to change the situation, he was beginning to focus on getting into the water and catching a few waves.

...sure would be good for my head...nothin' better'n getting into mother ocean and paddling away from the screaming anxiety of gray flannel humanity...brian wilson said it all...catch a wave and you're sittin' on top of the world...swell's half as good as it was this morning, still be some decent waves....

It was probably at the precise moment when he thought about going surfing that the idea of dropping out and hitting the road first occurred to him. It was the one thing he'd never done in his life. He'd always been as dependable as the sunrise down at the beach. When he thought back on his experiences, he'd done a lot, but he'd never been a drop out. The closest he'd ever come was in the fifties when he was a teenager. He and his buddies hung around The Unicorn on Sunset Boulevard and The Insomniac out in Hermosa Beach, but he was never irresponsible to the point of dropping out completely and hitting the road. He certainly had contemplated it a time or two in those days.

By the time the sixties rolled around, he couldn't even think about dropping out as he was focused on going to college and working part-time. He missed the whole hippy thing; he figured he was too old and his military training had made him too clean cut for that. He remembered seeing Jack Kerouac interviewed on some T.V. show a couple years before he died, and Kerouac had said something to the effect that the hippies were a bunch of bums, nothing like the beats, a point on which Soc agreed, though Kerouac's drunken patriotism during the same interview was off-putting.

So when a whole generation was turning on, tuning in, and dropping out, Soc was being the responsible young adult, going to college, getting educated, not because it would get him a better job, but to acquire knowledge so that he could make the world a better place.

The Death of Soc Smith

...oh well, so much for that plan...all i ended up doing with my degree was getting a job anyway, and i don't think i ever once used my education to make the world a better place...i was go'n'a join the peace corps and go to nigeria... good thing i didn't...not long after that, civil war broke out there over a place called biafra....

The one accomplishment that he could claim was that he'd brought a daughter into the world and raised her to be a good, responsible citizen. Certainly that contribution made the world a better place, but he hardly needed a college education to make it happen.

It wasn't long after they graduated that he and Jayne got married. They'd met in a Western Civilization class when they were both juniors. She went on after graduation, completed her fifth year and got a teaching credential. Then she taught at an elementary school for two years before she had Caroline. Soc had gotten a job in the rapidly growing electronics industry in Silicon Valley before it was even called that. The two years Jayne worked, they managed to save enough money for closing costs on a house they were able to qualify for and buy with his G.I. bill. They were in the house a year when Caroline was born. Jayne went back to work when Caroline started kindergarten.

Soc was the sole support of the family for those five years. He was locked in. Any chance he might have had to strike out on the road and get lost in America had long since passed. Thus, reconciled to the life he'd created for himself and his family, which really was quite good, he rarely entertained such thoughts. He loved Jayne and Caroline and was generally satisfied with his situation. But now the seed to ramble had been planted and was taking root, and he was beginning to think about the possibility of simply going along with the official consensus, which would certainly give him more freedom than he'd ever had in his life.

He headed down the freeway back into town and drove out to the beach. He didn't want to get his board and suit until he made sure the surf was holding up since he'd looked in the morning. As he crossed over the railroad tracks on the old wooden trestle bridge near the wharf, he looked left and saw some pretty good size waves rolling through the wharf pilings. As he passed the Dream Inn, he could hear them breaking on the rocks at the bottom of the cliff. With his first glimpse of the surf, he saw shoulder-to-head-high waves breaking from beyond the public toilet a hundred feet past the steps. He counted about thirty surfers out there.

It was so crowded that the parking places on all the side streets leading to the cliff were filled halfway down the block. He found a place on the circle right behind Max's fifty Ford Woody. Max, like Gillis, had been surfing Cowell's since the late fifties. He liked to tell people he first tried surfing with an ironing board, but Soc didn't know whether to believe it or not. He was an avid surfer, getting out at least four days a week. If the waves weren't breaking at Cowell's, he'd go over to some break on the east side. He was also an encyclopedia of surfing lore and legend, especially of the local surfing scene. He'd converted half of his garage into a surfing museum, complete with video tapes of *The Endless Summer, Big Wednesday, Gidget* and others. He had pictures of old-time local surfers with their gigantic fifteen-foot boards that were nothing but redwood planks. Max lived a block away from the beach. He'd set up his museum as a kind of social club where you could stop and have a cup of coffee after a long day of riding waves.

As Soc walked toward the cliff, he could see Max talking to Steve Genochio who was waxing his trademark red and black licorice stripe longboard. He called it his big licorice stick. He probably had a half dozen made over the years, and now you'd see some guy using one he'd bought used. When Soc got up close, Steve picked up his board and started heading toward the steps. Soc could see that the swell had picked up quite a bit.

"You goin' out, Max?"

"I think so. How 'bout you?"

"Yeah, I'm goin' out. Sets like these? Think Steve'll let us get any waves? He's a regular one-man crowd, that guy."

"Sometimes you got'a be aggressive. With him it's just a game of intimidation. You know, the funny thing with him is he can be the nicest guy you'll ever want to meet when you're talking to him up here on the cliff, but in the water, he's a royal pain in the ass. You off today?"

"Yeah."

That was a good enough answer for Max who didn't say another word about it as he headed toward home on foot, and Soc went for his car.

Soc pulled Jayne's car into the garage and shut the engine off. It took him ten minutes to get his surfing gear loaded into the Woody. Then he quickly went into the house and changed out of his suit and into a

The Death of Soc Smith

pair of trunks and Levis and a T-shirt. Slipping into his go-aheads, he crossed the patio and got back into the car. As he was pulling away from the house, the mailman walked up the front steps and deposited some envelopes into the mailbox.

...maybe i should stop and see what came in the mail...fuck it...i can wait till i get back ...probably won't be much for me anyway...i'm dead....

When he got back to the beach, the waves were even bigger than they'd been just a few minutes ago. Clint and Bart had gotten out of the water since their morning session. Now they were coming back for more. Leonard had also gotten out, but he wasn't back. Max was already in the water. Jesse was getting into his wetsuit. Soc talked to him as he got into his. Then he waxed his board and followed Jesse to the steps. It was getting closer to high tide, so he had to hook up his leash at the bottom of the stairs. The beach was completely submerged, and the waves were breaking over the lowest steps. It was unusual for there to be good surf with such a high tide. He paddled out and joined Clint, Bart, Max, Jesse and a lot of other surfers in the lineup.

He managed to get out without any waves breaking on top of him, and as he approached the lineup, he could see Max and Steve going for the same wave.

...max doesn't mind the hassle of taking off with steve...he makes it a challenge...and steve doesn't really give max a hard time like he does other surfers....

Soc always made it a point to avoid any waves that Steve paddled for. When he got to the lineup, he sat up on his board and rested. He was out of breath from paddling out. He rested through the whole set, preferring to wait for the next set. As he sat there, a sea lion poked its head out of the water about ten feet away.

...what cool animals these guys are!...

"How yuh doing, buddy?" Soc said, using the tone he used with the cats.

His big black eyes stared back at Soc, all innocence. Suddenly his shiny trunk curled back under the water, and he slid silently away.

A set was forming, and Steve still hadn't paddled back out, so Soc maneuvered to a spot where he thought he could catch the second wave, which he could see was going to be a good one, possibly the wave of the day. Clint had gotten back out, and he was going for it too.

The Death of Soc Smith

...be cool to ride this one with clint...he's mellow....

They both got up on it at the same time. Soc was in the slot and Clint was right behind him. He'd peek over his shoulder periodically to make sure he was staying ahead of Clint. When they hit the deep spot, they both turned slightly left to stay in the curl. Then it picked up again, and they raced toward the beach. Clint kicked out first, and twenty-five yards farther on Soc kicked out, too. He was completely exhilarated.

He lost count after his fifth wave. It had been just what he'd needed to take his mind off his situation. He hadn't thought about any of the day's earlier activities since he'd gotten in the water. It was almost high tide by the time he was ready to call it a day. He'd gotten a lot of rides during the session, and now he was feeling refreshed and tired at the same time.

...my money nothing'll revive a corpse like a good day's surfing...if i was dead before, i'm damn sure alive now....

So, he struggled with numb, cold hands to get his wetsuit off. Jayne would be home from work by now, so he was looking forward to getting there and telling her about the weird day he'd had. He'd purposely not called her earlier as he'd promised simply because the only news he had was bad news, and he wanted to give it to her in person, not over the phone. So now he braced himself as he drove home.

Eleven

Jayne was watching for Soc as he pulled into the driveway, and she came out through the patio gate to greet him. She was holding an open envelope as she approached him getting out of the car. He could tell from the look on her face that she was upset about something. When he got out of the car, she handed him the envelope and said,

"What's the meaning of this?"

He saw that it was addressed to her, and looking at the return address, he saw that it was from his life insurance company. It was open; he pulled out the contents. There was a letter and a check for fifty thousand dollars. The letter, also addressed to Jayne, explained that the check, made out to her, she being the beneficiary, was the death benefit from his life insurance policy. When he got to the part that explained the check, he felt his heart jump.

...maybe i am dead....

"Don't ask me," he replied. "I guess it's just something else to get straightened out, but judging from earlier today, I don't guess I'll be able to straighten it out any more than I was able to straighten anything out this morning."

"Why? What happened this morning? I notice you've been surfing. Didn't you work today?" Her voice sounded a little frantic.

"Look, why don't you go on back into the house while I put my stuff away, and I'll be right in to tell you how *my* day went. You won't believe it. I don't."

"Okay," she said and went back through the patio gate and into the house.

He took his wetsuit and board out of the Woody and set them down on the patio. Then he pulled the car into the garage and went back out to the patio and rinsed off the board and suit. He hung the suit on its hook and leaned the board against the garage. He rinsed off under the shower and walked into the bedroom drying himself as he went. He got into his sweat suit and walked into the kitchen where Jayne was fixing something to eat.

"Good news is I'm still alive; bad news is I can't get anybody to believe it."

The Death of Soc Smith

Her blue eyes were pleading, and one corner of her mouth curled slightly which usually meant that she was on the verge of tears. She felt completely impotent in this situation.

"Right after you left this morning, I called work to tell them I'd be late. Jim Jones from personnel came on the line and casually informed me that he'd heard I'd died, and he'd spent Saturday interviewing applicants to replace me. I didn't bother trying to explain that I wasn't dead. Figured I'd take care of it when I got there after I went to the county and the newspaper.

"I hung up and took off to the county. All I got from them was a lot of red tape and a big runaround. They told me they couldn't do anything about it, and, if you can believe it (I can't), they said that I should just carry on and not worry about any county death certificate. Really unbelievable. I just left, and when I got back to the car, there was a ticket on the windshield. Stayed too long in a one-hour zone.

"I drove over to the newspaper, but I didn't get anything from the editor but a lecture on the trials and tribulations of being a newspaper editor. His line was pretty similar to the one I got from the bureaucrats at the county. He basically told me to go to the post office and try to find out who sent him the registered letter authorizing him to print the obituary.

"Needless to say, after those two stops, I wasn't about to go over to the post office and get more of the same from them, so I went to the office. On the way I witnessed an accident at the Fishhook, so I stopped to lend a hand there. Some guy cut off another guy and he rammed into the divider. Then the guy who caused the accident just hauled ass on his merry way over the hill. I don't think the cops ever caught him.

"When I finally got to work, I found some young computer nerd cleaning out my desk, and when Josh and I went up to talk to Jones about it, he said he was keeping the guy in my job and he's transferring me to production and another job with Gillis. He gave me the rest of the week off, so I decided to go surfing, and that ended up being the best thing I did all day. So, how did your day go?"

Jayne didn't interrupt him once. She listened to him quietly, her outrage increasing after each episode of his tale. She had questions for every point he made, but she could see that it was useless to ask them because she knew the only answers she'd get would be what he'd already told her.

The Death of Soc Smith

"Soc, honey, what are we going to do? What if we can't get this thing straightened out?"

"I haven't even told you the worst part. Although they're telling me my job is secure, I have the distinct impression that they really want to ease me out. That's why the job switch may not be as good as they're trying to make it look. They sure didn't waste any time finding a replacement for me. And you should've seen that asshole Josh shrug when I tried to talk Jones into putting me back in my old job. Didn't give me any support. Should maybe start looking around for another job."

"But, Soc, if nobody thinks you're even alive, how are you going to get another job?"

"What do you suggest?"

"Call Rob Novak in the morning. This is a situation that calls for a lawyer. He'll know what to do."

"That's go'n'a run into some money."

"Well, you can't just be dead simply because some people have a paperwork problem. You've got some responsibilities here, and besides *you're not dead*."

"You're right and I know it. I'll call Rob first thing in the morning, see if he can do something about it."

"Boy, you should've seen the teacher's room at lunchtime. Everybody was talking about it. I couldn't give them any answers to their questions. Probably won't be able to tomorrow, either, looks like."

As they were talking, Jayne had started making chili. It was cooking as Soc went over and turned on the television news. Jayne set out two bowls, paper napkins, soupspoons and parmesan cheese. She popped the cork on a bottle of zinfandel and poured two glasses. She set them on the table along with the bottle. The last thing she put on the table was sourdough French bread warm from the toaster oven. Soc turned off the T.V. and sat down at the dining room table. Jayne started telling him about the work part of her day as they ate. She was exhausted just from trying to explain Soc's obituary to the other teachers.

They finished their chili and sat at the table savoring their wine. Then they picked up their dishes and took them into the kitchen to wash in the sink. After that Soc went out and hung up his wetsuit inside the garage and then he went for a walk downtown. Jayne settled down in front of the television and started to write some letters.

Soc pulled up a bar stool in the bar next to the bookstore at the north end of the

The Death of Soc Smith

Mall and ordered a Perrier. There were a few people sitting at the tables scattered through the back of the place. There was only one other person sitting at the bar, a woman up by the front window where the bar forms an ell. She looked at him until she got his attention. When he finally gazed in her direction, his glance was greeted with a smile. He turned quickly and looked at his own reflection in the mirror behind the bar. He wasn't sure what the smile meant, so he kept staring straight ahead as he thought about his next move. When he glanced her way again, she was still smiling and beckoning him with her right index finger to come and join her. His curiosity was piqued so he picked up his Perrier and moved up to that end of the bar and sat down opposite her on his side of the ell.

"Hi, I'm Rebecca. I work in the county office of vital statistics. I was there this morning when Dorkas was giving you such a bad time. She was the sour puss who was making life miserable for you. I was working at a desk right behind her."

...i was so baffled i didn't see anybody working behind the cement lady...i might've guessed her name would be something like dorkas...you'd think i would've noticed someone as pretty as this one....

Jerome Arthur

"I don't remember seeing anyone but the old concrete block I was dealing with."

"Good description. She has a way of consuming all of your attention by making you so furious that you can't think of anything else."

"Well, she certainly did that to me."

"What was the problem? Have a death in the family and some of the information on the death certificate was inaccurate?"

"Something like that. The only problem is I'm the member of the family whose death certificate they messed up on."

"But you're not dead."

"That's right, but try to convince old concrete face of that. Try to convince the newspaper of that. Try to prove it to my boss. I'm beginning to think that maybe I *am* dead."

"Well, it could be an opportunity. I mean just think about how free it makes you. You could disappear and start a whole new life somewhere else. In a way it's like being reborn."

...there it is again, only now it's coming from a neutral and disinterested party...but where would i go...always thought it might be nice to go back home to southern california...that'd be impossible...couldn't

The Death of Soc Smith

afford it...and besides, it'd be like going back home...if i'm go'n'a do something like that, i should go someplace new, someplace that I don't know, and where they don't know me...méxico!...that's it, baja...last year jesse went there on a surfing trip...said it was great...good waves, warm weather...sleep in the woody, surf my days away...who knows...might be cheap enough to rent a shack on the beach....

"Is there someplace you'd like to go that you've only dreamed about but never thought you'd take the chance and just go. I think that's what I'd do if I were in your position. I always wanted to go to some tropical paradise, Hawaii, Tahiti. If I were ever declared dead, I think I'd just up and go."

"The thought has occurred to me a time or two today. I've never done anything like that before. Always been pretty much on the straight and narrow. Went into the Navy, went to college on the G.I. bill, got married, bought a house, raised a family. Now that I've done all those things, why not run away from home? That's what I've been asking myself all day. Although, I am still married. Kid's all grown and on her own. House is paid for, but what about Jayne?"

Rebecca didn't answer that question. Rather, she sat silently sipping her drink. Finally she said,

"Look, if I can be of any help back at the office, I'll do whatever I can. In fact, when I go in tomorrow morning, I'll pull your file. Maybe there's something I can do that'll keep you from dealing with Dorkas."

"Hey, I'm grateful for anything you can do. Right now, all I am is just another corpse. I'm go'n'a talk to a lawyer friend of mine in the morning. See what he might be able to do."

They talked for about a half an hour, and Soc was ready to get out of that saloon-smelling environment and get going home. After draining his glass, he stood up and said good night to Rebecca. In parting he told her he'd be in touch with her the next day. He was home in twenty minutes to find Jayne sound asleep on the floor in front of the television set. He turned the set off, woke her up, took her to bed.

Twelve

Soc was awake the next morning by five-thirty. Baja was really on his mind. In fact, he began to think of different scenarios for getting some cash and getting out of there. He'd be leaving Jayne in pretty good shape with fifty thousand dollars in life insurance money. If he took ten of the twenty-five thousand cash that he'd been saving in the metal file cabinet in their closet, a fund they'd started right after Caroline went into kindergarten, she'd still have sixty-five thousand dollars.

...she ought'a be able to make it with a nest egg like that...makes good money...the house is paid for...'nother ten years, she'll have a good retirement...all she's got'a worry about is utilities, taxes and groceries...won't have any trouble at all hangin' onto the fifty grand...i'm dead...now all i got'a do is get buried...alive in baja california....

No sooner did he think these thoughts than he would banish them and start thinking and planning as he'd done before the obituary in the paper, before the death certificate from the county, before the death benefit from his life insurance. He thought about Jayne and Caroline and how he could possibly explain it to them. It was simple; he couldn't. As he lay in bed sorting out these possibilities, Jayne was sound asleep beside him. One of the cats was curled up between them at the foot of the bed. The gray light of dawn was just beginning to filter through the drapes that covered the sliding glass door. He heard a car go by out in front, and as it passed, he also heard the newspaper plop on the front walkway.

...what the hell...i mi's well get up and read the damn paper....

He got out of bed and put on his sweat suit, slipping into a pair of Birkenstocks as he pulled the elastic banded cuffs of the sweatpants over his heels. Parker, his youngest cat, his baby tom, jumped off the bed and followed him out the door and back in again.

...damn cat heels like a dog....

When they came back into the front room, Soc bent down to scratch him behind the ears, but as he reached down, Parker

The Death of Soc Smith

dropped to one side and rolled onto his back. He stretched his front legs out straight and purred as Soc scratched his stomach and chest.

Parker was his buddy, unlike the other cat, a ten-year-old female named Obsidian who resented Parker since his arrival a year ago. She'd always been standoffish with Soc. Oh, she'd arch her back and snuggle up to his arm when he was putting food in her dish, but most often she scurried away when he entered a room where she was lounging. He thought of her as Jayne's cat. As he tossed the paper onto the dining room table, both cats took their places next to their food bowls, so before making himself something for breakfast, he gave each of them a handful of kibbles. Then he fixed himself a bowl of cereal and read the paper. Parker climbed up and became a warm ball of fur on his lap. When he got to the page with the tide chart, he noticed that low tide that morning would be at nine o'clock and it would be a minus tide again at 1.4. The sun was just then peaking over the rooftops across the street.

...looks like another beautiful day in paradise...wonder if the swell's still coming through...maybe go surfing after i talk to rob....

Jayne came into the dining room. She leaned forward and kissed Soc's bald spot and hugged him from the back around his shoulders. Then she went into the kitchen and started packing her lunch and making herself some breakfast. He read through the sports section and comics and petted Parker as Jayne read the front page and ate her toast and cereal.

"I think I'll go check out the surf. Go'n'a be a good low tide at around nine, and if there's any kind of swell, I'm goin' out."

"You think that's a good idea? I mean, don't you think you ought'a be doing something to get this death business cleared up?"

"Like what? Did enough to last me a lifetime yesterday. I'll call Rob, and we can get together when I get out of the water."

He went into the bedroom and put on a pair of trousers and a shirt and went back into the dining room and told Jayne he'd be back in a few minutes. Then going out the back door, he crossed the patio to the garage and got into the Woody.

At the cliff, he stood watching the waves breaking on the sandbar that had washed down from the north coast. This pro-cess repeated itself every year at the start of

The Death of Soc Smith

the winter storms. When it was like this, people would lie on beach blankets down there. It would all be scoured out and washed down the coast to the river mouth and the yacht harbor as spring turned to summer.

His eyes moved from the sandbar out to the surf breaking in slow rolling "ankle snappers" as Jesse called them. It was a calm morning all blue and gold across the water. There were a few surfers out, and from where Soc was watching, it looked like perfect conditions for small, fun waves. It was still only about seven-fifteen, forty-five minutes before he could try calling Rob.

He watched for about fifteen minutes, got into the Woody, and headed back home by way of the point. As he drove around the point at Indicators, he was looking at perfect lines of shoulder-high waves coming around the point at the Lane. As he neared the lighthouse, he ran into a traffic jam. Surfers were scurrying everywhere trying to get to the action while it was happening. As soon as he passed the lighthouse, the road was clear, and he was back at the house by twenty to eight, just in time to kiss Jayne goodbye. After watching her and Betty drive off down the street, he went out to the garage and put his board and wetsuit in the Woody. He put on a pair of cut-offs and got on the phone and called Rob.

"Hi, Soc," Rob said when he came on the line. It was just eight o'clock. "You caught me at a good time. I'm going to be in court all day, and I just stopped by the office to pick up some briefs. So, what can I do for you?"

"You know about the obituary they printed on me in the paper last Saturday, right?"

"Yeah?"

"Well, I can't seem to get it straightened out. Also, Jayne's received a death certificate from the county and a fifty-thousand-dollar check from my life insurance. I've talked to the county and the newspaper, and I can't seem to convince them that I'm not dead. I don't know, I just thought maybe you could help me out here."

"Of course, I can help you out. I can get the county to void the death certificate, and the newspaper really should print a retraction. Can you come in at nine tomorrow morning? Bring all your documentation with you: the death certificate, the newspaper article, and whatever you got from the life insurance company. We'll get going on it right away."

The Death of Soc Smith

"All right, Rob. Thanks a lot. I'll see you in the morning."

"See you then, Soc."

When he'd hung up, he headed out the back door, scratching Parker on the neck as he went.

He was aware of how quickly things were going as he hustled down to the beach. It was like that every time when he'd go surfing. He'd think about it in what seemed like slow motion, and once he made up his mind to go, his pace picked up gradually until he was going so fast that he thought he was racing when he finally got into the water. And then once he was in the water, as often as not, he'd straddle his board sometimes for as long as forty-five minutes waiting for a wave.

When he pulled onto the cliff, he could see that the swell had picked up. The waves were breaking from knee to waist high. He didn't even bother to look at the waves again before suiting up. He took the board and suit out of the car and started to get ready. He waxed his board, locked the car and headed toward the steps. It was about a half hour before low tide, so the sandbar was high and dry. Soc walked to where the surf was hitting the sandbar, fastened his leash to his right ankle, and walked into the water.

Jerome Arthur

...this is looking good...nice 'n' glassy, and just the right size....

None of his friends were in the water, but he recognized most of the people who were out. They were regulars here whenever there was any kind of swell at all. Soc stayed to himself and spent the next three hours catching five to six waves an hour. By eleven-thirty most of the other guys were in the water. The swell just kept building, so that by the time they got in, the waves were waist to chest high. It was a picture-perfect day, sunny with a slight breeze, and surfing conditions just got better and better as the swell picked up. As the waves got bigger, the water's surface got glassier. Soc got several rides all the way into the beach from outside, and all he had to do was get into the slot and ride with the minimum of maneuvering on the board. He could walk to the nose and back at his leisure.

"Which Gidget was a pro ice skater and did all her own surfing in the movie?" Max was asking Bart as Soc paddled back into the lineup after one of his rides. As Bart thought about the answer, Max paddled around him and about ten feet beyond, and turned his board around quickly and started paddling for a wave.

The Death of Soc Smith

"You know, he only asks those questions to distract you so he can beat you to the waves," Clint told him. Bart still had a puzzled look on his face as if he were still trying to figure out the answer to the question. Max was back soon enough, as he'd only stayed on the wave for about twenty feet before losing it. When he got back to where Bart still waited for a wave, he said,

"Deborah Walley. She even once rode a surfboard wearing ice skates...."

That was all that Soc heard as he was paddling into a wave both of them missed seeing, but Max was asking yet another question. Once he was up and riding, he looked over his shoulder and saw Max and Clint paddling into the second wave in the set as Bart watched. With every ride, Soc was now debating whether to go in or stay out. He'd had a big day, more than his share of waves, but he just couldn't bring himself to get out of the water.

Thirteen

When Soc paddled back out to the lineup, he saw Jesse and Billy hanging with Bart.

"How long you guys been out?" Soc asked when he got close enough.

"I just got in," said Jesse.

"I got in the water at about ten-thirty," Billy said. "Was out at Indicators for the last hour. Thought I'd come join you guys here at Cowellskiki. Checked out the east side before I came over here."

"What was it like over there?"

"Tide was too low when I looked, but I bet it's doing good right now. I might go over there when I leave here. Catch it at medium high tide. This south swell keeps up, it should be perfect then."

A wave was taking shape about twenty feet beyond them. Soc and Billy got into position and started paddling for it. Billy was

The Death of Soc Smith

out front, Soc right behind him. The wave picked up the tails of their boards and they were off. They didn't go twenty yards before a helmeted kayaker dropped in on Billy, and just as he did so, he went out of control, and his kayak careened along sideways in the wave. Soc kicked out as soon as the kayak got on the wave, but Billy, who hated "butt surfers" passionately, didn't, opting instead to ride the wave, which he considered to be his own personal property. There was no collision, but Soc could hear Billy cussing the kayaker for the next fifty feet. Billy's voice was drowned out by the crash and hiss of the breaking wave. Paddling around it, Soc headed back out to the lineup.

"Billy just had a run-in with a kayaker," he said to Clint as he got back into the lineup.

"Oh, Jesus. You'd think kayakers'd know better. He hates those guys. What happened?"

"I's right behind him on the same wave, and this kayaker drops in on him. I kicked out, so I didn't catch what went on after that, but Billy was cussin' up a storm. You know how he gets."

"Good wave you guys got. Too bad the kayaker wrecked it for yuh."

There was a lull between sets, and everybody gathered in groups of three and four. Billy paddled back out shouting how he'd taken care of the kayaker. The guys were all watching him and joking with him as he as he got closer to the group.

"Won't have that gay faggot to worry about anymore today," Billy said. "Got in my way. Nose of my board punched a hole in his kayak."

He laughed raucously. The other four joined him. Soc cast his gaze to the beach where he saw the kayaker carrying his boat over his head as he moved toward the steps.

"I'm going back out to Indicators," Billy said. "I was out there for over an hour and didn't hassle with a single kayaker. Anybody wan'a come with me?"

Soc and all the others said they'd stay right where they were. Billy paddled off by himself.

...i remember too well how big and fast those waves can be...last time i went out there, i almost died...first wave i caught was like an elevator ride...i was going down so fast, i couldn't get off my knees...all i could do was hold onto the rails and drop faster than i ever dropped before or since...i hit the trough and got back down on my stomach and turned out after riding only about ten

The Death of Soc Smith

yards...next wave i paddled for was about a foot overhead...got right into the spot where i thought i'd get a good ride...damn wave closed out on me right when i was on the crest...went over the falls, and forgot to take a breath before i went under water for a long time...spin cycle...don't think i could've stayed under much longer'n i did...came up gasping and fighting for air...when i finally got back onto my board, all i could do was lie there and gasp...started throwing up, and kept on all the way back into the beach...had'a stop the car twice on the way home 'cause i had'a barf....

"I'm half tempted to go out there with him," Bart said. "Some good waves out there."

"Not for me," Soc said.

"I know what you're talking about," Clint said. "I'm stayin' right here. 'Sides, those guys out there are all young. When you're over fifty like us, you tend to be careful."

The next wave Soc got, Jesse was already riding. It slowed a little as it moved from inside Indicators to outside Cowell's, and Jesse was hanging in there when it picked up again. That's when Soc got onto it, and it was a long ride in all the way to the beach. This is when he finally dragged himself out of the water. It was three o'clock. He wanted to be at the house when Jayne came home from work. Jesse, Clint and Bart got out around then, too. At the top of the steps, Soc laid his board down on the double-railed redwood fence along the cliff and watched those who were still in the water. Leonard was riding his left. Max was taking the same left in and heading for the stairs. When Soc got his breath back, he picked up his board and trotted across the street and then walked the half block to the Woody.

Betty was getting out of Jayne's Buick as he came around the corner and approached the house. As Betty was getting into her car, the two women waved. Jayne pulled her car into the garage. As she lowered the door, she glanced at Soc and looked away.

...oh well...guess she's still pissed 'cause i went surfing 'steada' taking care of that other business...i'll take care of it tomorrow....

She went out of the garage through the side door and into the house. Soc took care of his surfing things, rinsed off under the shower, put on his sweats, and joined her at the dining room table where she was reading the mail. He threw the clothes he'd worn to go surfing into the washing machine.

The Death of Soc Smith

"Any more surprises in the mail?"

"No, but here's a letter from my mother."

"Oh, what's new over there."

"She's complaining about daddy's drinking. Apparently, he can't hold it anymore. Starting to have mood swings."

"What a drag."

"Did you talk to Rob?"

"Yes."

"What did he say?"

"I'm meeting him tomorrow morning at nine. Way he talks it's not go'n'a be a problem."

"Well, good."

"Said he c'n get the county to revoke the death certificate, and the paper to print a retraction."

"Good," Jayne said, a little too hastily. This quick, forceful response almost seemed like a sermon to him, and if there was anything he wasn't in the mood for just then, it was a sermon. "I'm glad to see things'll be cleared up so we can get back to normal."

"Yeah, me too, if for nothin' else just to mellow you out. You been stressing, and when it's done, I'm hopin' you'll lighten up."

"You act like you've been unaffect-ed?"

"Not really," Soc replied. "I knew it'd get straightened out sooner or later."

"It would only get straightened out if you were going to do something about it, and a couple times there, you acted like you didn't care one way or the other."

He didn't respond, but he was think-ing he liked the freedom that death was giv-ing him. And the silent pressure he felt from her was driving him in search of it. But now all he had to do was go see Rob Novak in the morning and it'd be taken care of.

"You'll never know how much I cared about getting it straightened out. Would've been nice to stay in my old job."

"Oh, you'll be able to handle the new one, especially considering the raise they're go'n'a give you."

"I suppose. I'll go up Friday after-noon. Check out my new office."

"Good idea."

"Meanwhile, if the swell holds up, I'm goin' surfin' every day for the rest of the week."

"Okay," Jayne said. "I think this'll be a positive move in the end."

Fourteen

The swell did hold up through the rest of the week, and Soc went surfing every day. He went to Rob's office on Wednesday morning. He watched as Rob dictated into a hand-held device three different messages, one to the county, the second to the newspaper and the third to the insurance company. He told Soc not to worry, that everything would be taken care of. After he left Rob's office, he went home and changed the radiator hose on the Woody. Then he went surfing, and he got into the water every day for the rest of the week.

At the end of his Friday session, he left the Woody out, and after he rinsed his gear and himself off, he went into the house to tell Jayne he was going up to check out his new digs at the plant. Then he hopped in the car and headed toward the office. Since the rush hour was gearing up, he decided to take surface streets instead of the freeway. The speed limit was only twenty-five, but he figured traffic on the freeway wasn't moving much faster at that hour. When he got to Scotts Valley, he took the bridge across the freeway and pulled into the company parking lot. It was ten to five and the parking lot was still full. Soc found a spot in the visitor's section and pulled into it.

He went in the side entrance of the building and walked down the corridor to the end. Turning left he was walking toward two large swinging doors with shiny bands of metal running across the bottom. The black plastic sign above them had white lettering that said, "Production." Soc had been down here before, but not often, and the first thing he noticed as soon as he passed through the swinging doors was the noise level. He hadn't remembered it being so loud the few times he'd been here. He was in a huge room with about four different assembly lines working. Not only was it loud, but this workplace was also very busy. The room was a jumble of organized chaos. Soc was looking around for Gillis but couldn't see him anywhere. He walked around a bit, unnoticed by the workers who were intent on their jobs. Just when he was about to tap someone on the shoulder and ask after Gillis, a buzzer sounded and various people on the lines went around throwing switches, and the machines began to shut down. The other workers were heading toward the swinging doors. Soc stopped one of them.

"Excuse me. Is Gillis around?" he asked.

"Try his office back around the corner there."

Before Soc could ask another question, the worker was gone, so he walked back in the direction he'd been sent and found a row of four windowless offices along the wall. The first office was empty, its occupier having covered up her computer terminal for the day and moved her chair neatly into the kneehole of her desk. In the second office, he found a woman securing her space for the day.

"Hi," he said. When she looked up, she was distracted and acted put out by Soc's greeting, annoyed at being detained. "Is Gillis anywhere around?"

"I don't know," she replied. "If you don't see him, I guess he's not. I haven't seen him since about three-thirty myself. His office is not this next one, but the one after that. Now if you'll excuse me, I've got an important engagement at five-thirty, so I'd like to get out of here."

Again, Soc didn't have a chance to ask another question, the woman having slipped by him and walked around the corner and out the swinging doors. By now the whole production department was deserted. Soc went to the next office and looked in, only to find that it was empty save for the boxes of his things that the young guy had packed on Monday in his old office.

...must be where they plan to put me...there's my stuff....

He moved on to Gillis' office and found it deserted like the rest of the area. Gillis' desk was cluttered with papers and books, but it looked like it was as straight as it ever got. It looked like Gillis was gone for the day, so he left the area and went back to the office where his things were stored. He grabbed the box and headed up to take one last look at his old office. The only people in the place by now were the night watchmen and the custodians. Josh wasn't in his office either. Soc went to his old office and looked in. It was somebody else's office now. Not one thing of Soc's remained, not even the aura. His entire career was packed into the box he was holding in his hands. He headed back out of the building and over to his car.

...down to serious stuff now...honestly don't know how i'm ever go'n'a work in

The Death of Soc Smith

that dungeon they call production...i couldn't believe those offices...no windows...and all that noise...quiet now, but it won't be come monday...how'm i go'n'a fit in here?...where's gillis?...guess it's time to start thinking a little more seriously about baja...always wanted to do something like that, but was too straight and narrow to ever attempt it...'member when i was a senior in high school and i's having all that trouble with my dad?...he used to get drunk a lot and yell at me a lot for not having a job...i got a job and got so pissed off that i thought about moving out of the house and renting a room in one of those flea bag hotels downtown...but i never did...instead, i was dependable, kept living under his roof, staying in bed until after he'd go to work, and then get home from work late at night after he'd gone to bed in a drunken stupor...yeah, i stuck it out, old reliable soc...and then the military...did my duty for my country...just lucky there wasn't a war goin' on at the time...stayed consistent...went to college...got a career...got married and had caroline...been living the american dream ever since...dependable soc smith...now's my chance...caroline's grown and jayne's got a secure future...nothing to stop me now... what a cop out!...i mean, doing it after you've gone through all the motions, and after you've been declared dead...zero risk... got to be done...can't stay here, cop out or not...and so what?...even if it is a cop out...something I always wanted to do... now's my chance...maybe should've done it back in the time...monday soon as jayne and betty leave, load the woody up with some clothes, sleeping bag, surfing gear...last thing i'm doin' before I leave, grab some of the cash from the file cabinet, get on the road....

Fifteen

Coming down off the hill on the freeway, Soc saw the waning light of day over the bay. The cities to the south, a handful of jewels scattered along the beaches that bordered the foothills of the mountains, were just beginning to sparkle in the angle of the descending sun across the shimmering water. It was really a beautiful view, one of many he'd seen over the years that he'd been living here, one that he would miss as much as he'd miss Jayne. Having made up his mind to go, he was experiencing conflicting feelings of sadness and resolve. Twenty-five years was a long time for any two people to live together. He reckoned that not many of his contemporaries could boast the same longevity, and now he was preparing to put an end to it, but he wasn't just leaving his marriage. He was leaving his life, and it wasn't his fault. Someone else made him dead. That, at least, was going to be his rationale whenever he needed to justify what he was doing.

He was catching the tail end of the rush hour. The traffic was at a standstill at the intersection where the shopping center was located. It took some time getting home, and by the time he pulled into the driveway, it was six-thirty. Before he went into the house, he moved the box of his personal things into the garage. He opened it and took the pictures of Jayne and Caroline out of the frames. He put them in the glove compartment of the Woody. Then he lifted the hood and checked the oil and the water level in the radiator. Both were in good shape. The new hose he'd replaced Tuesday was looking good, too. No leaks there. He dropped the hood and wiped some grease off his hands with the rag he'd used to check the oil. He tossed the rag over into the corner on top of an old, rusty hamster cage.

...caroline's last hamster...eleven years ago...still in junior high...given to her for her birthday by one of her school chums...couldn't believe that a kid would give another kid something live like that for a birthday present...jayne ended up taking care of it for the two years it lived, and when it died, she left the cage in the service porch for about five years, and then somehow it got

The Death of Soc Smith

out here...don't know how we missed taking it to the dump last time we went....

Leaving the empty cage in the darkness of the garage, he headed across the patio and into the house. Jayne was watching the evening news on television and writing a letter to her mother. He was glad that she didn't immediately question him about his trip to the plant. He thought he'd be too nervous to give her a straight answer. As soon as he entered the house, his heart started beating faster, and he was aware of a certain excitement from knowing what he was about to do, and also knowing that he couldn't speak out about it, thus rendering anything else he might say for the next forty-eight hours a lie. He sat down and watched the news until the next commercial came on, and when he got up to fix himself something to drink, Jayne asked him about his new office.

"It was actually kinda' hard to tell. I couldn't find Gillis anywhere, and everybody cleared out right at five o'clock. By ten after, I found myself all alone in a deserted production department. In fact, the whole plant was deserted. 'Cept for the cleaning crew. I went looking for Gillis up front, but he was nowhere around. Couldn't even find Josh, and it's unusual for him to get out of there before five-thirty. I never saw him do it in all the years I worked for him. At first, I thought they both might be upstairs in Kingland's office, but when I got back out to the lobby, the parking lot was empty. Cleaning crew's van, the Woody and the night watchman's pickup truck were the only cars out there. I'll catch up with them on Monday."

A pang of guilt shot through him, and he trembled slightly as he uttered this last. He realized that he was lying to her. He knew damn good and well that he wasn't going to find out any such thing on Monday. He did know that he would be on the highway heading south, trying to put as much distance between himself and that job as he could. He'd also be putting distance between himself and Jayne and Caroline, and that thought made him feel sad and lonely.

He fixed himself a glass of orange juice and went back into the living room and watched the news with Jayne. He was making a mental inventory of some of the things he wanted to take with him. He was figuring which of all his lightweight clothes he wanted to take.

...summer's coming...go'n'a be hotter'n hell down there...should take a good jacket, too...don't know how cold it's go'n'a be come winter...think i'll head for la paz...bet it's plenty warm there...or maybe

The Death of Soc Smith

san josé del cabo...bet they got a good point break there....

He walked over to the bookcase, got out the Atlas and turned to the page that showed México. Then he got out a Triple A map he had of Baja California. It looked like San José was a better spot for surfing than La Paz, but he wouldn't know for sure till he got there. He put the book and map away and watched the news.

When he looked to see what Jayne was doing, he noticed that she was alternately watching the news and writing her letter. At times she'd look at her writing, holding it away at arms length, looking at it as she thought about what to say next. Then her gaze would shift to the television screen where smiling, pastel people were dispensing the polyester news. Soc looked at them, but he wasn't hearing anything.

...colors don't even look real, for cryin' out loud...nobody's skin looks that color ...guy's ears're whiter'n his face....

He got up and went into the bedroom where he spent five minutes opening and closing drawers and looking at what he had hanging in the closet. When he came back into the living room, Jayne was watching him as he came through the hall door, watching him as though she'd been listening to what he'd been doing.

"Is there something wrong, honey?" she asked. "You seem antsie."

"I'm okay. I'm just disheartened by what I saw in the production department this afternoon. It's noisy as hell, and no windows. All florescent lights. Hell, on a sunny day, I didn't even need to turn the lights on in my old office. Got enough light from the one window I had."

"At least they're paying you more. There's some consolation in that. Maybe when you see that extra money coming in, you'll tend to forget about the other stuff."

"Yeah, maybe you're right. Boy, the surf sure has been good the past couple days," he said by way of changing the subject, not wanting to talk about the other any longer. "Seems like the swell just keeps building. I think that freak storm we had last Friday is what's causing it. It really stirred things up."

"There've been quite a few cars parked along the highway at Four Mile the last couple days."

"Yeah. Imagine it's good up there, too."

Soc watched the news through the sports report. He went into the bedroom and

The Death of Soc Smith

changed into some clothes for an evening walk. When he came back into the living room, the news people were signing off and so was Jayne on her letter.

"If you're going for a walk, can you mail this letter for me?"

"Sure."

"Thanks."

He hugged and kissed her and walked out the front door. Putting the letter in his hip pocket, he started off toward downtown.

Sixteen

Soc deposited the letter in the mailbox that stood next to the front door of the post office. Descending the stairs, he walked across the street, past the war memorial and into the bar he'd gone into on Monday. It was quiet. He found a place at the bar and ordered a Perrier and a twist. No one was sitting at the bar; the only other people in the place were three couples sitting at tables toward the back by the door that opened onto the patio. One couple was out in the patio. As Soc sat sipping his drink, the door to the lady's restroom swung open and Rebecca came out.

"Oh, there you are," she said and sat down on the bar stool next to him. "I didn't know if I'd ever see you again. You didn't come back to the office on Tuesday."

"Nah, went surfing instead. Been out every day this week. Got some great rides."

The Death of Soc Smith

"So, you're a surfer, too? Get your problem straightened out?"

"Not really. My lawyer's working on it."

"I looked at your file, and it looked to me like all it would take would be a memo up to the C.A.O. I went ahead and sent one off. Guess we'll find out soon enough if it worked or not."

"To be honest with you, I don't even care anymore. I'm thinking about bailing outa' here, and it may happen pretty soon, too."

"Oh, I'm sorry to hear that. I was hoping maybe I'd found a new friend, and now you're already leaving."

He made no response, so they sat in silence staring at their own reflections in the bartender's glass.

...damndest thing...hardly ever go into bars...never been in this one until just last Monday...probably shouldn't come to any hasty conclusions here, but i'd swear she'd take me home...for the asking....

Another guy came in and pulled up a bar stool near the front window.

"Where are you planning to run away to?"

"Oh, I was just kiddin'," he lied. "I'm not goin' nowhere. And even if I were, it

131

wouldn't be smart to be telling anybody about it. If I did that, I'd never be able to get completely away from my past."

She didn't quite know what to say to this, so she simply looked at his reflection in the mirror and said nothing.

"So, is this a regular hangout of yours?" Soc asked.

"Oh no, I don't hang out in bars. Monday was my first time here. I only got here fifteen minutes before you tonight. And I only came back on the odd chance I'd see you again. I wanted to tell you what I did about the memo, and I wanted to see you again."

"Monday was my first time here, too. I've seen this place from out on the street and always wondered what it was like inside, so I came in."

"Look, why don't we cut the small talk, and go over to my place. I've got some Perrier or just about whatever else you'd care for."

This direct advance took Soc aback. Things like this didn't happen to him. In fact, he wasn't sure he could remember it ever happening. He was aroused. He thought about it for a minute or two, and he still couldn't give her any kind of response. She

The Death of Soc Smith

finally took his hand as she got off her bar stool and began to pull him forward.

"Wait a minute," he said, not releasing his hand from hers. "I can't just walk out of here holding hands with you and get into your car and drive off. I *am* a married man, and I should be a little more discreet than that. You go ahead to your car, and I'll follow you."

"Okay my car is the green M.G. across the plaza on Front Street."

"Okay. I'm right behind you."

He sat back down as she left. He quickly downed his Perrier, got up and was out the front door before she'd crossed the plaza. He followed her around the corner of the bakery, and there was her green M.G.B. He waited for her to start the motor before he climbed in beside her. Sitting in this little roller skate of a car, he suddenly became aware of his age. The little car was comfortable enough; it was just that he felt like he'd fit in better if he was twenty years younger. She zipped off down the street, and he felt like a kid again, riding on his Flexi down the sidewalk.

...don't feel like I'm sitting much higher in this rig than I was on the flexi, for sure...feel like my butt is riding right on the street....

She turned left two blocks down and headed east.

"You're go'n'a bring me back here later, aren't you?"

"Don't worry about it."

"I can't exactly stay out all night, you know."

"I know. I'll take you to within a block of your house before midnight. You can stay out that late, can't you?"

"I guess."

Her place was only about a half mile away, so he was less concerned about whether she'd bring him back or not. He could walk home from there in less than an hour. She lived in an old garage converted into a one-room cottage with a bathroom off to one side. Along one wall was a table with two chairs, one of which was not accessible because it was wedged between the wall and the table. She offered him the other chair, and he sat down.

"Would you like a beer or something?" she asked.

"I'll take or something. What might that be?"

She didn't say a word. She walked over to where he was sitting and leaned over and kissed him on the mouth, raising him to his feet with her firm hands flat against the

The Death of Soc Smith

sides of his neck and jaw, the same strong hands that had tried to lead him out of the bar earlier. Almost before he knew what hit him, Soc was in bed making crazy love with this young woman, thirty years old at most, whom he'd only met five days before.

They stayed in bed until eleven o'clock, three sessions of love making interspersed with conversations about various topics from Soc's recent woes to Rebecca's life story. At eleven, he got dressed as she lay in bed trying to coax him into staying a while longer. When she could see that he was going to go whether she drove him or not, she got out of bed, too, and got dressed for the drive back across town. He didn't let her take him all the way back to the house. She dropped him off two blocks away, and he made sure she was long gone before he walked the rest of the way home. Jayne was sound asleep, and the house was dark except for the nightlight they kept on all night long in the living room. He closed the bedroom door, got some dental floss from the bathroom, and went into the living room and watched Johnny Carson do his monologue while he flossed his teeth. He was in bed by a quarter to twelve.

Seventeen

He slept soundly until four o'clock when he awoke just as a sweet dream drifted off into the ether.

...wow! what a beautiful beach and i'm all alone here...must be baja...perfect waves breaking, one after the other...two other guys in the water...they ride endless perfect waves...grab my board and get in with them...first ride's a tube ride...in the green room now....

And he couldn't even tell if it was green or not. His dream was in black and white like an old movie. When he came out of the tube, his board shot out from under him, and he splashed into the water, waking up in the process. The water splash of his dream continued in his waking consciousness as a storm hammered the patio awning with rain. Like voices whispering loudly in the night, the downpour murmured against the patio and the fences surrounding it.

The Death of Soc Smith

He lay awake for a few minutes, staring at first at the ceiling, and then turning onto his side and watching Jayne breathe softly in her sleep.

...looks so peaceful, completely oblivious to the kind of shit that's about to go down...maybe she knows a lot more'n i think she does...might've read my mind...maybe she'd just as soon i go...i'm goin'...i know i'm goin'....

He closed his eyes and fell asleep. When he opened them again, it was six-ten, the rain had stopped, and Jayne was pulling herself out of her side of the bed. As she entered the bathroom, Soc sat up in bed and put his feet on the carpeted floor. He was getting into his jogging suit in the dark light of early dawn when Jayne came back into the bedroom and turned on the bright light on the ceiling rather than the softer one on the nightstand, and its brightness jolted him.

...last time that'll happen....

He slipped into his Birkenstocks and went out and got the morning paper. The damp sidewalk and street glistened under a dark gray sky. He looked at the western sky and only saw more gray. Approaching the front porch, he saw Parker peering out over the kick plate of the screen door. When Soc opened the screen, the cat quickly ran out and disappeared up the side yard of the house.

The only thing that interested him as he skimmed through the paper was the tide chart. There was going to be a -0.3 at two-fifteen that afternoon. As Jayne came into the kitchen after her shower, Soc looked up from the paper and said,

"Wan'a go get some breakfast at Tip-Top."

"Sure. You going surfing today?"

"Low tide's not till two-fifteen this afternoon. Little early to be looking right now. We could go check it out after breakfast. Sure, yuh wan'a go?"

"Absolutely."

With that Soc went into the bathroom to take his shower. When he came out, Jayne was finishing a cup of coffee and the morning paper. They went out to the garage, and he got the Woody out. They pulled into the parking lot behind the restaurant. They didn't see anybody they knew. They sat in a booth by the window and watched the traffic go by as they ate in silence. They hadn't talked about Soc's death and all the problems related to it since yesterday. And they weren't talking about it there at the breakfast table.

They went down to West Cliff after breakfast to check out the surf. It was still

The Death of Soc Smith

early, and the tide was still high, but the swell that had been going all week, was holding up even when the tide was a little high. The waves weren't breaking right then, but he could see that as the tide went out, it was going to be another great day. He drove home, and he and Jayne lounged for the rest of the morning.

At one o'clock, he loaded the Woody with his board and wetsuit, and headed down to the beach. When he pulled out onto the cliff, he saw Clint's and Jesse's pick-ups and Billy's V.W. bus all parked in the turnout, and when he got past the guard rail, he could see the three of them in the water going for waves. Leonard was surfing his left. The swell hadn't abated, but the wind had, so the water was smooth as glass. It was a perfect calm after a storm. The sky was pale blue and as still and quiet as a sleeping baby.

...if i was ever go'n'a get a barrel ride here, it would be today...look at 'em...must be five footers....

No sooner did the idea cross his mind than he saw Bart getting tubed. He got his board out of the car and put on his wetsuit. He surfed till almost four o'clock. He was all refreshed and feeling great. He had a big smile on his face.

Eighteen

On Monday morning he was up early, filled with anticipation for what he was about to do. Jayne got up right behind him and followed him into the bathroom. He went into the kitchen as she got into the shower. He sat and drank his coffee. He could hear her rustling around in the bathroom, taking her shower, blowing her hair dry, putting on her makeup. He couldn't stop thinking about what was about to go down.

...so this is what it all comes down to after twenty-five years...i'll hug and kiss her goodbye, and it'll be the last time i do it....

Jayne gathered up her school things, and before she could go out the door, he stepped in front of her and took her in his arms and gave her a long hug and kiss.

"Whoa. What brought that on?" she asked. "See you later."

His "goodbye" was lost in the swirl of wind that followed her out the door. He

The Death of Soc Smith

went into the bathroom and got the hot water going. He got dressed after his shower and laid out seven changes of clothes. They were all casual clothes that didn't need to be hanged on hangers. He folded them, putting them in the suitcase he usually used when they went on trips. Then he went out to the Woody and put his suitcase in the shotgun seat. He loaded his surfboard and wetsuit in the back. The last thing he saw inside the garage as he was closing the door was the rusty cage with the rag on top of it. He went into the house and unlocked the file cabinet. He dug out the cash envelopes from the back of the bottom drawer. There were five, each with five thousand bucks in them. He took two and put the other three back.

In the kitchen he found the pad that Jayne used for making her grocery lists. He tore off the top sheet and sat down at the dining room table and wrote:

Honey,

I'll be gone by the time you get home today. I love you. Remember that always. I just can't stay here any longer. I don't know what to do to get my life back. I guess, nothing, so I'll just be on my

way. I must be dead. I love
you.

Soc

He was now set to get going. He took one last look around the house. It was a nostalgic moment for him, remembering all the good times he'd had here with Jayne and Caroline. This was the house they were living in when Caroline was born. He and Jayne had raised her in this house. He turned and went out the back. He had to get out of there before he lost his resolve.

He double-checked everything to make sure he wasn't leaving something behind that he was going to need later on. Finally, he put the carrier on the rear bumper and mounted his bike on it. Now he was sure he had everything he needed. Then he went back into the house and scratched and petted the cats and said goodbye to them.

Before he headed out of town, he drove down by the beach for one last look at the swell. As he passed by his regular surf spot, he could see that Max, Leonard and Steve Genochio were all in the water. He drove past the Dream Inn on the bluff straight out to the freeway and headed south.

The End

1990-2019

About the Author

Jerome Arthur grew up in Los Angeles, California. He lived on the beach in Belmont Shore, a neighborhood in Long Beach, California, for nine years in the 1960s. He and his wife Janet moved to Santa Cruz, California in 1969. These three cities are the settings for his ten novels.

CPSIA information can be obtained
at www.ICGtesting.com
Printed in the USA
FSHW022039210820
73199FS